A MIDDLE WAY:

The Secular/Spiritual Road
to Wholeness

DUKE ROBINSON

DEDICATION

I dedicate this book to Spiritual Secularists everywhere. By steadfast vision and faithful actions, they seek to bring both the warmth of grace and the light of truth to this cold, dark and dangerous world that so desperately needs them.

*The world is too dangerous for anything but truth
and too small for anything but love.*

William Sloane Coffin

ACKNOWLEDGMENTS

Authors do not produce their books alone. They are inspired, provoked and often guided by others. Such folk, in enlightened conversations, give them ideas, support them, or challenge their thinking. I owe a debt to many teachers, colleagues, congregants, students, and friends with whom I talked over the past six decades about the issues in this book.

I'm especially indebted to five independent thinkers who care about both truth and me: Bob Anschutz in Michigan, Paul Gertmenian and John Hadsell in nearby Oakland, Richard Golden and Doug Hergert, who live in the same retirement community I do. They went through the entire manuscript, some more than once, and gave me encouragement and honest, constructive proposals regarding the text ... some of which I followed. Doug also was the indexer for the book.

Thoughtful friends, Vernon Alexander, Eric Anschutz, Marilyn Barulich, Bobby Frankel, Paul Fillinger, Milton Matz, Ian Harris, Lou Satz, Ben Slomoff, and Jane Walter read particular portions of the manuscript and raised questions that prompted minor but important changes to the manuscript.

My gratitude also goes to Molly Williams, who created the cover, and to Jim Compton for his proof reading and light copy editing.

Lastly, my thanks go to Claire Blue, the love of my life. She always responded honestly to what she read, not only when my efforts weren't clear but also when she liked them. I deeply appreciate, too, her willingness to endure long periods of time the past year when I was physically present but out-to-lunch mentally--the inevitable absentmindedness of authors when living inside their books.

So who is responsible for any shortcomings of this book? You get only one guess.

CONTENTS

PART ONE: GETTING OUR BEARINGS

CHAPTER 1: THE TWO BASIC TERMS

CHAPTER 2: WHAT MAKES US SO SPECIAL

CHAPTER 3: YOUR TAKE ON THINGS

PART TWO: VIEWING WHAT WE INHERITED

PART THREE: SORTING OUT THE ISSUES

CHAPTER 9: THE BATTLES OF SCIENCE

CHAPTER 10: ON BEING FULLY SECULAR

PART FOUR: TAKING A REWARDING ROAD

CHAPTER 11: SECULAR SPIRITUALITY

CHAPTER 12: SECULAR SPIRITUALITY VS. CHRISTIAN TRADITIONALISM. . . . 165

A bit beyond perception's reach I sometimes believe I see
That life is two locked boxes, each containing the other's key.

Piet Hein

No matter how thin you slice it, there will always be two sides.

Baruch Spinoza

Catch a cold and do nothing about it; and it will last a miserable two weeks. Drown yourself in drugstore over-the-counter remedies or take your doctor's prescriptions faithfully, and it will hang around for a fortnight. But, if you immediately will get down on your knees and pray fervently, God will cure you of it in 14 days.

Unknown

INTRODUCTION

When the early nineteenth century German poet Goethe was about to die, he reportedly cried, "Light, light, what the world needs is more light!" Years later, the Spanish philosopher Miguel de Unamuno announced, "Goethe was wrong. What he should have said was: Warmth, what the world needs is more warmth. We shall not die from the dark, but from the frost."

Both men were right and wrong. For us to survive and be authentically human, or complete, or whole, which is our goal, we need an abundance of both light and warmth. We can die from either the dark or the frost.

In America, two powerful worldviews battle every day for your loyalty. The old one comes from the Bible. It claims that a supernatural God created and controls everything. Along with His angels, like a caring father, this God will answer your prayers, work real miracles, and take care of you as His child. In this life, this ancient worldview offers you the *warmth* of a spirituality rooted in relationship with this God. For the afterlife, it offers a warm reception in heaven.

The second and newer worldview belongs to science. It is *secular*, in that it concerns itself only with the physical, natural realm of this life. It includes no supernatural God, no angels, no miracles, no afterlife. It claims to offer the *light* of truth about our universe's origins and human nature, based on verifiable evidence.

I fully support neither of these worldviews. Each of them offers something important, but each fails to lead us to both the important *light* of truth and the authentic *warmth* of spirit.

Whether you're aware of it or not, you have your own worldview, or philosophy of life. It may be it was drummed into you as a child, or over the years you've built it fairly carefully, or you've thrown it together haphazardly. It may have been shaped by either the biblical or the scientific worldview, or both. Whatever the case, it's your unique take on things. Think of it as the mental framework that can hold your life together, or the lens through which you focus on the most critical of human issues. And know that it gains value by how accurately you answer such questions as these: "Where did everything come from? Why is life such a predicament? What will it take for me to live my best possible life?" When your worldview nails down important truths and provides the warmth of authentic love, it supports your pursuit of wholeness.

A major battle has been joined, because the findings of science have shed light on many of the great mysteries humans always have longed to understand and have even thought they did, but didn't. For many free-thinking people, these findings have eroded confidence in the Bible's worldview and have rendered appeals to God and the supernatural world needless and, at points, deserving of ridicule. An increasing number of Americans are elated by this erosion, and many enjoy discrediting religion.

A large majority of Americans, however, still believes in angels, miracles, prayer and a God who will take them to heaven. Many are miffed at scientists and science for undermining their beliefs. They also are frightened. They believe that to lose their faith would make God angry at them. Others feel that if they reject religious ideas they were taught as children, they'll be betraying their parents. Believer parents of younger children are anxious at the thought of not helping them feel special and secure in God's arms. And many believers of all types are afraid to give up the warmth and certainty of their faith without having something satisfying to put in its place. I've worked through that fear and can understand their anxiety and hesitancy.

This book addresses those on both sides of the battle. I write to people who were reared in supernatural religion, or who at one time bought into it and remain there. At one level, their faith still may give them comfort in the face of life's hardships, including dying, an immediate social context and a sense of place in the larger human picture. But they now see the extraordinary achievements of science and feel the weight of its arguments against *supernaturalism*. To be intellectually honest, they may know they should drop their religion, especially if they still abide in it out of habit, or because of social pressure, or due to the fears I mention above, or simply for not knowing where to turn, but they sentimentally cling to it.

I also address those who can't stand what they know of religion but also are put off by narrow-minded scientists and arrogant atheists. I am not writing to reconcile science and religion—religious thinkers have been trying to do that since science began to change the Western World's view of reality. Rather, I lay out a road between the two, a realistic middle way that can help to ground, integrate, balance, and liberate thinking people to be authentic in the twenty-first century.

The book breaks down into four parts. **Part One** deals with what I do and don't mean by the terms *secular* and *spiritual*, describes a spirituality you find in your everyday, natural experiences, and argues that we are different from the other species mainly by virtue of this spirituality. Next, you will find brief summaries of twenty belief systems, or worldviews, followed by the challenge to develop your own take on reality in light of our painful human *predicament*—the inescapable contradictions and limitations of our humanity that imprison us all.

Part Two sheds light on the historic struggles of Christianity and on how it continues to dominate America's thinking about spiritual matters. It describes how secularization and secularism, in the last half-century, have shaken the country's once widely shared Christian worldview, and then looks at how other age-old religions in America understand spirituality today. A transitional section explores the stunning, mind-shattering findings of science, which have forced us to rethink what is real about the universe and ourselves.

Part Three assesses the battles in which science finds itself embroiled with its enemies—and also with its friends, among whom I count myself. It then hangs out to dry the dirty laundry of science, denounces *scientism,* or the zealous worship of science, identifies the difficulty of developing badly needed ethics for today, both personal and global, and explains the import of the provocative New Atheists. The concluding chapter discusses how and why responsible scientists check their haughtiness.

Part Four lays out the case for a middle way I call *Secular Spirituality*. It first explains how Spiritual Secularists in general answer our three critical worldview questions: "Where did everything come from? Why is life such a predicament? What will it take for me to live my best possible life?" It then details how those who associate themselves with Christianity in some way, as I do, deal with the disgraceful self-invalidating views of Christian traditionalism. A following section outlines how to check for authentic voices that claim spiritual reality, and how to discern which spiritual paths might deepen your sense of wholeness. Part Four concludes by describing the values, attitudes, commitments and behaviors of people who do a good job of being fully secular and fully spiritual, and whom I admire.

If too often you seem to be slogging in sand; or you feel fractured due to holding onto scientific and religious worldviews at the same time; or sometimes you want to scream because your brain seems locked and you don't feel intellectually free; and these ills have stunted or killed any joy in your life; and you do not want to live the rest of your days this way, I encourage you to read further. If you have trouble with either narrow-minded science or traditional, supernatural religion, or both, the middle road I invite you to take should lead you to the kind of wholeness the unifying principle of *Yin* and *Yang* in Taoist philosophy represents.

Millions of pages have been written on these subjects. I don't expect to answer fully the questions I try to address. I draw on philosophy and theology, disciplines in which I have formal training, and whose limitations I clearly see. I am not a scientist by profession, but I reflect on a number of the sciences, particularly physics, biology, anthropology and cosmology. I see the strengths of science and its shortcomings, too.

This book is not an academic work, and you will not need an advanced degree to stay with me. While I offer no footnotes and few references to sources for statements or people I quote, however, I do expect you to mull over what they and I say and, whenever anything strikes you as a bit fishy, to check it online—Google it—for clarification or opposing views.

This book is not for the close-minded or fainthearted. The fact that you have read this far tells me you are not afraid to think, you can handle whatever rings of truth here, and you hope to find the pages ahead a source of knowledge and personal growth. At the least, I trust that any thoughts and feelings this book evokes will put you on the road to more light and warmth, to a deeper sense of being whole.

PART ONE
GETTING OUR BEARINGS

I don't believe in astrology. I am a Sagittarius, and we're very skeptical.

Arthur C. Clarke

The only thing certain is that nothing is certain.
If this statement is true; it also is false.

Ancient Paradox

It is not the brains that matter most, but that which guides them—the character, the heart, generous qualities, progressive ideas.

Dostoyevsky

That's a spiritual lifestyle, being willing to admit that you don't know everything and that you were wrong about some things. It's about making a list of the people you've harmed, either emotionally or physically or financially, and going back and making amends. It's not a fluffy, ethereal concept.

Anthony Kiedis

CHAPTER 1:

THE TWO BASIC TERMS

Softening the Tough One

Not long after I graduated from Wheaton College in Illinois, a former classmate stunned me. He said that in our student days he'd seen me as "extremely secular." The school we attended is known for its piety and petty morals as well as academic rigor. (*Time* magazine once referred to it as "the Harvard of Evangelical colleges.") He was trying to compliment me for not being pious. But I was annoyed, because I thought *secular* was a dirty word that didn't apply to me. It took me a while to realize how wrong I was on both accounts.

Here in the first chapter, I want to explain what I mean by the terms *secular* and *spiritual*. The first task will be relatively easy. The second will be much harder, because the term *spiritual* has been so abused that its negative associations are turnoffs to so many of us. I wish that I had a better word to capture what I am talking about, but I don't. So, it is important that I explain what I am and am not talking about when I say *spiritual*. If we understand its positive connotations they can help free us to take a middle way and find the wholeness we need living in the real world.

Here is the easy part. Secular has to do with the *seculum*, the material universe, this planet, nature, and us as physical beings. Serious scientific secularists hold that the cosmos, though dynamic and beautiful, is cold and without meaning. They insist there is no credible evidence of a God, or of we humans being the beloved children of God. They tell us the evidence is overwhelming that we are animals. Most people believe that *secularism* is cold.

I contend that, if we are not the special glory of God's creation as the ancient writer of Psalm 8 declares, we are a staggeringly different marvel among marvels, a complex, inexplicable mystery that cannot be captured completely under the designation of animal. I shall be arguing that we are so radically distinguished from other life forms on the evolutionary trail that we best know ourselves not by our similarities to other creatures but by our radical differences, which are profound. We'll look further at this in the next chapter.

Secularists are mainly known for not wanting government and religion to get into bed together. They argue that whenever in Western history this has happened, the two have conceived grotesque offspring in terms of policies that oppress the citizenry. We all know that one of our government's major concerns is Middle East countries controlled by religious extremists. They try to establish religion-dominated theocracies rather than secular democracies. Yet serious secularists think most of us are asleep with regard to scarey attempts by Roman Catholicism and Protestant fundamentalism to control what happens in this country. I don't agree with everything secularists stand for, but I feel fortunate that my country is an official secular democracy and not a theocracy.

Hard-core secularists, many of whom are atheists, tend to be hostile to all religion. They view belief in God and claims to revealed truth as superstition and a stumbling block to human progress. They see religious faith as a cop-out in the quest to understand the origins of the universe and our humanity. They admit that we do not and cannot know everything, but they reject the notion that we should use supernatural forces to explain things we don't understand. So do I.

Orthodox Jews, fundamentalist and evangelical Christians, and traditional Muslims all see hard-line secularists as enemies and often speak ill of them. Those of us who have broader sensibilities, both religious and nonreligious, agree with certain things for which secularists stand: we affirm their scientific view of the universe, their criticism of narrow-minded, dangerous religion, and their concern to keep church and state separate.

Most secularists don't hate religion—they simply go about their business as if it is not helpful and God does not exist. In 2007, Pope

Benedict visited Spain. He took a hard line in charging lapsed Catholics there with "pretending God does not exist." They said they didn't see themselves "pretending" anything; they simply weren't taking seriously God, religion, or the pope. Like secular Americans, when they catch a cold they turn not to prayer but to pills, chicken soup, and hot toddies. If cancer strikes them, they are inclined to take the chemotherapy their secular physician prescribes and not pray for God to step in with a miracle cure.

Such behaviors do not necessarily come from a closed-minded, scientific or philosophical secularism. They can result simply from passing through the liberating "process of secularization," which almost everyone in this day has done, to one degree or another, whether they recognize and admit it or not. This process and a rigid secularism are two radically different realities, just like the fluid river and the hard rock that lies in its bed are not one and the same. We'll look further at the "hard rock" of secularism and the process of secularization in coming chapters.

Charles Darwin, in the nineteenth century, in his *Origin of the Species*, shook the Hebrew-Christian supernatural view of things when he established the foundation for evolution. Let me affirm right here that his discovery, with the overwhelming evidence to support it that science has found since his day, leaves no doubt in my mind that we are highly evolved animals.

Along with everything else in the universe we are a contemporary expression of billions of years of evolution. Our genetic makeup connects us to everything else—we are made of the same stuff as the stars. Of the three billion base pairs in the human genome, only 1.23 percent of them are different from those in the chimpanzee genome; koalas have fingerprints almost identical to ours (the same combination of loops and arches); geneticists have fused a human gene with a corresponding rodent gene; and years ago surgeons in Southern California successfully transplanted a baboon's beating heart into a man's chest. At the level of evolutionary biology, we are inextricably tied to the other animals. Science calls us biomolecular machines, quadrillion-celled animals.

Anthropologists and biologists place us in their broad category of vertebrates, with nearly 400,000 other species. With the other vertebrates we feature segmented spinal columns, brains enclosed in a cranium, instincts that fuel and direct our energies, and hearts that pump blood to muscles and vital organs, including our genitalia.

When it comes to class, we're mammals, comprising about one tenth of the vertebrate species. Our mammalian mothers bring us forth as living young rather than as eggs. As mammals, we drink milk from our mother's mammary glands, as do the offspring of other mammals such as cows, camels, water buffalo, horses, pigs, yaks, cats, dogs, and, yes, whales. Within the mammal class, we are placed in the order of primates, the smartest mammals, with proportionately larger and more developed brains. The more than 250 known primate species include apes, monkeys, baboons, mountain gorillas, and chimpanzees, animals all of us recognize. Scientists finally place us in the genus *Homo*, with the species name *Homo sapiens.* This narrowest designation marks us as the wisest of primate species, the "thinking primate," or "modern man."

We don't like to think of ourselves as animals, but we certainly can see physical similarities between the other primates and us. We're also struck by how we can assign personality to a fun-loving dog (Snoopy), a perky mouse (Mickey), an exasperating cat (Garfield), and even a charming sow (Miss Piggy). And we are impressed by the intimate companionship people establish with their pets and by the comfort they derive from them.

Scientists today, however, acknowledge that biology alone does not define our distinctive human nature. Cultural evolution stands on the foundation of biological evolution and plays a dramatic role in fashioning what we are like. This nonbiological evolution accounts for changes in our brains over shorter spans of time (centuries, generations, or decades rather than millions of years). These changes arise not from genetic information but from information we accumulate through experience, memories, relationships, schools, books, radio, television, and now the Internet.

This new, cultural information gets imprinted on top of genetic information implanted, or encoded, in our brains, and it changes us. Genes, hormones and other biological factors determine in broad outline the way we think and behave. But from the moment we are born, our brains are always changing. The fact that they are pliable and somewhat *under-determined* genetically has allowed us, and spurred us, to evolve into a special species. Of course, we are touching here on the enduring enigma that is the mind/brain connection and the old *nature vs. nurture* debate; and I say, in each case, it is not *either/or* but *both/and*.

Without resorting to the notion that we are children of a God in heaven, I contend we are distinctive and special among the animals by virtue of spirit. Other animals have their own glories. Think of the bloodhound's sense of smell, the eagle's vision, the owl's hearing, and the elephant's ability to detect rain still far away. These senses stand out as dramatically sharper than ours. Our glory is spirit, and it makes us not merely animals. We may be "a horse," but we are "a horse of a different color."

In my adult life as an active Presbyterian minister, and now in retirement, I've been secular and not what people think of as "religious." At the same time, I have seen myself as spiritual, though not in the way traditional religion pursues supernatural spirituality. I'll be talking about an alternative, natural spirituality, the elements of which are familiar and available to us, yet are too often taken for granted.

Where this spirit, or the spiritual, comes from is difficult to determine, and its existence is debated. I will argue, however, that this spirit is something real at the center of human nature and experience; and that it deserves to hold a basic place in your worldview. I also will press the point that once you have established it there, you owe it to yourself to keep in mind how it affects you and what it asks of you.

Hardening the Soft One

My focus in this book will be on spirit, the spiritual, and spirituality. Of necessity, however, I must talk about religion in general and Christianity in particular. None of us escapes the enormous impact of Church teachings about the supernatural. Its emphasis on worship, prayer, and other forms of piety, its views of human nature, a supernatural God who interacts with us, and life beyond the grave all profoundly affect how we all look at spirituality. To understand this impact today, we will review the Church's past and present struggles with the powers of secular philosophy and science. After that, we will look at both the glories and shames of science as we know it. All this will be background to understanding better how we look at spirituality and the significance of what I am proposing.

My affirmation of spirit tells you that I see us, in one sense, as *hybrids*, as both nonmaterial and material beings. Further, I view us as holistic, or multifaceted selves. In other words, we are more than just physical, or rational, or sexual, or social, or aesthetic beings; we are all these things, a myriad of interdependent parts that, working together, produce whole persons.

Those who take spirit seriously insist that human reality consists of much more than you see with your eyes, put your finger on, or put in a test tube. The religious among us, of course, believe that the "much more" is God and our relationship with Him. Without an appeal to the supernatural of the traditional Western religions, I share with them our critical need for the warmth of spirit.

All of us, for several reasons, have trouble saying exactly what we mean by spirit. Our five senses and rational minds, by which we know almost everything, don't seem able to capture spirit's nature. Even as I believe what I mean by spirit is essential for human wholeness, I have no language precise enough to define it—some insist that that is what spirit is: *the indefinable*.

We have tried a number of metaphors. Along with the biblical authors, poets and mystics have used *breath* to help us understand spirit. They say both are invisible and vital for our survival. Some use fire, energy, wind, and water as symbols of spirit. They do so because these elements, like spirit, often are moving, spontaneous, and not always controllable. Others speak of "a divine spark," or "a light within" to identify the energy we identify with spirit. Some may find these metaphors helpful, but in the end, I suggest that, like all of our best words, they fail to capture fully what spirit is.

It's also hard to be precise about spirit, because people use the terms *spirit* and *soul* interchangeably; some see them as one and the same. Most believe both refer to a consciousness higher than that of vegetation, though some think flowers have souls. Others use the terms to identify two different aspects of human consciousness. Still others use one term for humans and one for the other animals, as do I, even though they may use them in the opposite way I do. For the sake of communication, therefore, let me tell you how I distinguish between them: I see soul as the life-energy that animates physical bodies. This animation includes physical mobility, sensory awareness, instincts, and emotions. So defined, we and all the other animals are souls. We'll not really talk about soul again. We will focus on spirit.

The spiritual waters get further muddied because Christianity, Judaism, Islam, and Eastern philosophy, and their many different sects, fill the American air waves with talk of spiritual matters. Also, feminine, Native American, ethnic, and what we call *New Age* spirituality broadcast their perspectives. We might say that America is the Wal-Mart or Amazon.com of spiritual marketing.

Look at the varied items people put in their spiritual carts:

- **The supernatural:** The Gods of Judaism, Christianity and Islam, angels, demons, exorcism, miracles, unnatural healing, speaking in tongues, answered prayers, magic, and life beyond death.
- **Sacred places:** The awesome experience of entering temples, sanctuaries, cathedrals, gardens, museums, caves, or islands where miracles allegedly took place, mystics gather, or relics are kept.
- **Devotional practices:** Meditating, praying, doing yoga, studying scripture, singing and chanting in pursuit of personal peace, joy and a sense of oneness with everything.
- **Wonder:** The elation inspired by a fresh, unplanned glimpse of stunning beauty in a loved one's face, or by holding in your arms and staring into the eyes of the mystery we know as a newborn baby.
- **Beauty in nature:** Hawaii's rainbows, sunsets, and exotic fish, a perfect budding rose, shooting stars in the midnight sky, the universe itself that magnifies one's sense of awe, mystery or good fortune.

- **A sense of perfect connection:** The deep conviction that you are one with the universe, a particular place, an ethical purpose, a *soulmate,* yourself, or with your God.
- **Hope:** The energy you experience when, in spite of an awareness of evil, pain and death, you possess a satisfying picture of the future that enables you to face life confidently.
- **The inspiration in art:** Inner responses to the artistry of Michelangelo, Ansel Adams, Beethoven, or the Beatles, which lift your spirit and make you feel that it's good to be alive.
- **Unconditional love:** Undeserved acceptance from others or your God that makes you feel welcome, enriched, and complete, along with your hospitality toward others who haven't earned or merited it.
- **Enlightenment:** Heightened awareness, fulfillment and inner contentment that come from something you witness, experience, do, or learn.
- **A sense of calling:** The compelling conviction that you were born for important work that will serve and support your loved ones, others, the common good, or your God.
- **Courage:** the inner power that could cause you to fight, at risk to yourself, for such values as freedom, peace and justice.
- **Exotic experiences evoked by mystery, mystical marvels, the occult, or anything spooky or beyond the rational:** Dreams, altered states of consciousness, ESP, inner voices, Bigfoot, precognition and clairvoyance, mediums talking with dead people, Zen and Tantric sex, emotional alchemy, the *zone,* biofield therapies, hypnosis, auras, necromancy, synchronicity, *déjà vu,* holistic integrative medicine, the paranormal, ecstatic moments, the power of paradoxes, dowsing rods, crystals, peak experiences (*getting tired of the spiritual?*), multiple orgasms, parapsychology, telekinetic abilities, ancestor

worship, hallucinations from using LSD, numerology, sacred relics and icons, channeling, UFOs and extraterrestrials, aromatherapy, *feng shui*, the energy generated by dance, controlled breathing, tarot readings, trekking the Himalayas, prophecy and fortune telling, (*will this list ever end?*), Ouija boards, palm-reading, astrology, candlelight, incense, homeopathic medicine, magnetic healing, time travel, astral bodies, out-of-body and near-death experiences, levitation, poltergeists, past-life regressions, Elvis sightings and messages, stigmata, the face of Mary on a pizza, telepathic trances, *chakra* development, seances, chi, witchcraft, faeries, wizards, and, yes, Satanism, werewolves, Voodoo, zombies, vampires, goblins, Gothic tales, sorcery, curses, hexes, spells, jinxes, and the summoning of ghosts that generate an eerie inner terror.

Do we live in a psycho-spiritual Disneyland, or what?

Having read this list, do you have any feel for where you stand on the spiritual scale? To get a good idea, go back over the list and draw a line through the items you believe are phony, superstitious, insignificant, or simply silly. What about seances? Angels? Do vampires and zombies cut it? Do they deserve to be crossed out? The fewer items you put a line through, the higher you are on the scale. If you are not certain about what you think of an item, put a question mark by it; you can come back to the list later.

I ask you to do your own thinking. But you cannot believe a particular item is real simply because most people do—we all know the masses often are wrong, and conventional wisdom can be extremely unwise. We don't need absolute proof that something we cannot see or measure is real. But when anyone claims something is true that lies beyond the self-evident or rationally provable, we must ask for some kind of evidence. We'll come back to this, and before the book is done we'll review a few criteria you might use to check the veracity of claims to spiritual experience. At this time, I urge you to be hard-nosed with the items

I listed—some have proven not only foolish but also fraudulent, even dangerous.

As you may have discerned in reading the Introduction, I stand low on the *spiritual scale*. A lot of the supposed manifestations of spirit people believe are real, I do not. I'm attached to those I can say are real, with the consent of all of my faculties. I am, therefore, doing away with miracles and angels, and prayer geared to change the mind of a God up in heaven. I can hear the charge: "Take these away from some readers and you will rob them of hope, as you would were you to shut down all the state lotteries on addicted gamblers. You also are in danger of killing for some a lot of mystery, magic and fun in life—like telling children there is no Santa Claus." But let me be clear that I am not writing to children; and I am only telling readers what they already know, if they will stop and think about it and will be honest with themselves. While I take away the supernatural I point to an abundance of mystery and beauty and hope, and a love worthy of awe, adulation and joy in our natural world. If their faith is mainly what gets some readers through life, I offer them a new way of seeing what it means to be human; and I operate on the assumption that most of them will be far better off being in touch with the real world and their real selves.

In that long list of supposed spiritual powers, some were considered to be good and some evil. As for evil, I know there are dark forces that damage us, such as traumas, phobias, compulsions, addictions, psychoses, chemical imbalances, and character disorders. I see them, however, not as supernatural but as natural. I do not believe that either angels or demons are real. When Roman Catholic authorities and Voodoo priests speak of demon possession, they are talking about wicked, supernatural spirits. We all have heard people speak about a troubled person's *demons,* usually referring to besetting addictions or mental illnesses. When we stop to think, however, we all must admit we have no evidence for the reality of supernatural creatures, and that this is an archaic, unscientific way of identifying negative powers in us that we don't understand or don't seem able to control.

Secular Spirit

When I speak of the spiritual, I am talking about natural experiences that energize us with joy, nourish us deep down, lift us high, and call out the best in us. To be spiritual is not to profess dependence upon, or interact intimately with supernatural powers but to respond to the truths and love that make us genuinely human, that help us be real persons who embody and generate light and warmth.

I suggest that spirit prompts us and then invades our experience whenever we

... forgive ourselves and others who fail or violate us;

... create something beautiful that we and others can enjoy;

... take off on adventures that broaden our horizons;

... affirm ourselves as physical and do things to keep fit;

... are kind to someone who is needy and hurting;

... express gratitude for someone's kindness to us;

... do something to help the vulnerable support themselves;

... share a meal with someone, and it's more than food;

... get free from the burden of preoccupation with ourselves;

... apologize to someone whom we've offended and hurt;

... realize what enriches us and express our gratitude for it;

... newly align with projects that generate peace with justice;

... take care of someone who needs our loving hospitality;

... see our imperfections and still like and accept ourselves;

... rightly receive validation from someone important to us;

... undergo tough times with others and form bonds with them;

... celebrate times, persons and experiences that benefit us;

... process the pain of grief and go on to live with hope;

... are touched by someone's courage, or compassion;

... make love (having sex simply is a secular experience);

... experience a breakthrough with what to do with our lives;

... hear someone say, *I love you*, and we know they mean it;

... do something that helps bring order out of chaos;

... ask meaningful questions that turn a light on in our brain;

... hear a call to do something important and we answer it;

... go through adversity and find valuable meaning in it;

... gain an insight that shows us how to be better persons;

... are drawn to a new commitment to serious learning;

... feel freed to use our skills in work we love to do;

... decide to use our time, energy and resources for good;

... pursue our passion even though physically exhausted;

... hold a newborn and become elated over the *magic* of life;

... sacrifice for others in crises with no thought of reward;

... act in ways that make us feel more fully ourselves;

... bond with a loved one who knows he or she is dying; or

... try to come to deeper terms with our own mortality.

Whenever we do the right thing with conviction and passion, particularly when at cost to ourselves, our action creates positive spiritual energy in and around us. People worldwide find that the right thing to do is to treat everyone with respect, support what is most just, restore dignity to those abused and oppressed, and help provide safety, security, freedom, and peace for themselves and others. When you or I give ourselves in some way to such endeavors, we feel spiritually whole; that is, grounded, integrated, balanced, and liberated. So while I am talking about a *natural* spirituality, it packs remarkable power.

Sometimes spirit awakens in us deep appreciation for what other people do or say. For example, when they throw their arms around us, accept us as we are—especially when such favor is undeserved—and they stand with us through thick and thin, spirit gives birth to strength, elation and hope in us; it makes us feel real.

When friends or coworkers freely join with us in an important endeavor we enjoy a *chemistry* with them that makes us feel, we say, like *family*. From my perspective that is spirit enriching us. It's like what we see in team sports; when the members put the team before themselves—a universally honored practice—they inspire us, and we all feel right about both them and their play, even if they lose.

When a musical group performs a beautiful piece, or a powerful song with great tempo and solid beat, their music and the other listeners' responses touch us deeply, perhaps to tears, or they make us clap our hands, or tap our toes or jump from our seats, spirit has awakened and taken us over. As our elation is fed back to the performers, it triggers more vitality and self-giving in them, and when this in turn stirs us even more, they pick it up and get higher *in the groove* or *in the spirit* so we all are transported by the emotion to pure joy—it's a spiritual experience (in contrast to enjoying the same piece on tape that's been recorded perfectly in a sterile, empty studio).

When nineteen firefighters personally and professionally plunged into the 2013 Prescott, Arizona firestorm, and heroically died, trying to save their community, it was spirit that called out their commitment. And then, in respect and gratitude, spirit flooded the hearts of their families, friends and those they were protecting, people who will never forget their ultimate sacrifice.

When oppressed peoples, holding the vision of a better life, at risk to their lives, defiantly and nonviolently rise up in the attempt to throw off their oppressors, we Americans, because of our history, find ourselves deeply touched, and we honor their leaders as heroes. The stories of Gandhi, Martin Luther King, Jr., Nelson Mandela, and many others will forever inspire us.

These brief accounts of what I am calling spiritual experience leave us with several not-so-easy questions to answer, which we will try to do in the next chapter.

We can easily forgive a child who is afraid of the dark. The real tragedy of life is when adults are afraid of the light.

Plato

What are humans that you are mindful of them, mere mortals that you care for them? Yet you have made them little less than a god, crowned them with glory and honor.

Psalm 8: 4, 5

It's what you learn after you know it all that really matters.

John Wooden

I do not feel obliged to believe that the same God who has endowed us with sense, reason, and intellect has intended us to forgo their use.

Galileo Galilei

CHAPTER 2:

WHAT MAKES US SO SPECIAL

Marks of Our Uniqueness

A growing number of materialists, those who see our incredible brain as the source of everything we are, insist that spirit is unreal and that we are merely highly developed animals. I'm convinced it is important to counter this secular, narrow scientific view, because of the spiritual richness I have experienced of our remarkable nature, and of what I see of spirit's importance for your life and mine and for the well-being of our species.

Certainly, because of spirit human beings are not merely animals. It clearly is the *vital principle* of human nature that makes us *Homo sapiens* stand out from the other animals and transforms us into full-blown *persons*. We see a number of differences between ourselves and other species in relation to our spiritual consciousness, differences we must understand in terms of contrast, not comparison. Some striking divergences from our closest kin, the chimpanzees, are clearly *quantitative* in nature. In other words, certain of our important features simply are dramatically more developed in us than in them. But we cannot fail to recognize that the most *notable* divergences are so great that we can take them as *qualitative*. We differ from them to such a degree, that the differences, for all practical purposes are in *kind*.

Consider with me a few essential differences between us and the other species. First, we humans engage in mental activities of which other animals are incapable. We think trains of thoughts, grasp the abstract, are aware that we are aware, become enlightened by encounters with the world, can be logical, are able to communicate what we think, enjoy telling and listening to stories, make choices based on consequences, and tap into beauty and mathematics. No other animal knows two plus two equals four, let alone anything about geometry, cosmology, or neurobiology. To set up a debate about this claim with the smartest representatives of any other species would be unfair, and, proving my point, actually impossible.

As we consider our uniqueness, we must not reduce our brain-mind activities simply to rationality. Among the glaring differences between us and other animals is that we have a radically different emotional makeup. We've not always recognized this. The notion that our big brain is simply a reasoning machine goes back to Aristotle. But today, neuroscientists tell us brain scans give clear evidence that our feelings as well as our thoughts are products of the same indivisible system. And our feelings, they tell us, include not only the bold contrasts of love and hatred but also a multitude of nuanced emotions in between. They say that emotions are central to our experience as the chemicals in our brain react to the 2,000 bits of information it processes every second. Exactly how our thoughts and feelings interrelate, they don't presently know; it's one of the many mysteries about us. At the same time, it's clear that emotionality proves as important to our human experience as rationality. It's equally evident that while members of certain other species may have some strong feelings, they are nowhere near as subtle, complex, or richly diverse as ours.

We are compulsive creators. Far beyond making what we need simply to survive, we boast marvelous technological inventions to make life easier and bring us pleasure. We've invented air travel, photography, dentistry, space satellites, microcomputers, and smart phones, to name just a few. We have crafted sophisticated tools to decipher the genetic codes and map the brains of all animals, including our own. We create myriad forms of architecture, fashion, fine arts, and music to generate beauty, reflect mystery and enrich our living. To survive, birds make nests, beavers build dams, spiders weave webs, ants carve underground catacombs, and monkeys use sticks to dig for termites to eat. But their works pale quickly beside our creative accomplishments. Again, I am talking substantive contrast here, not comparison.

Unlike the other animals, we thrive as individuals. We say *I, me, my,* and *mine,* assuming a particular someone is at home inside us (a self living behind our eyes)—a self-conscious person living in and dependent most immediately upon our brain. We realize that while it appears to us that we are separate selves, we now know that in reality each of us is connected to everyone and everything else, and that we have no independent existence, or fixed essence — we are neither singular nor static. In other words, we are constantly changing in dynamic relations and have no static *being* that affords us essential independence. At the same time, we sense deeply that our primary, lifelong task is to get to know better and relate more respectfully to that person whom we identify as our self, and then to every other person who touches our lives.

This is an important thought for your worldview. How do you see *yourself* in relation to everyone and everything else? Think about it. There is no doubt that you have a measure of *dependence* (the lean-on psychology of childhood); you also have a measure of *independence* (the break-free psychology of adolescence); but as an adult your fitting psychology is *interdependence*—you live as one who came from, and still are connected to, all else that is. You neither are self-made nor by yourself self-sustaining—such view of the personal identity has been a popular but false American myth. But so is the idea that it doesn't matter whether you grow up and take as much responsibility for your life as you possibly can.

Many factors establish your identity as a person: genes, name, gender, race, age group, personality, temperament, birth order, sexual orientation, body type and size, religion, nationality, subculture, language, education, worldview, art, standards of beauty, habits, sexual orientation, what you eat, social mores, and more. They affect how you think of yourself. Not so with other animals—their gender, dominant sexual orientation and species traits alone define what they are and how they act. To establish your identity, your parents gave you first and middle names—they didn't want others to confuse you with anyone else. Have you noticed that we name our pets, but, as far as we know, they neither name themselves nor refer to us by our names?

We humans have developed more than six thousand languages. With the help of language, we as individuals establish our identity, create intimacy, maintain relationships, carry on business, and form complex communities to support and guide us. Other animals have not developed sophisticated language, so they cannot, as we do, negotiate complex, mutually beneficial arrangements with one another. Animals do communicate within their groups to let other members know what they want—things like food, sex and shelter. Yet to benefit not just ourselves but society as a whole we negotiate and abide by thoughtfully designed social contracts, such as traffic signals, speed limits, and driving on the same side of the street.

We live with an eye on the future. In his book *The Selfish Gene,* evolutionary biologist and author Richard Dawkins, writes that "one unique feature of man, which may or may not have evolved ... is his capacity for conscious foresight." The past, present and future tenses of language help us reinforce our memories, establish our identities, tell our life stories, inform our dreams and nurture our will to live. We all sense that we have a potential to actualize, a unique self to develop and be, and we will be fulfilled only as we abide by what it takes to grow and mature as persons. All the while, we also are painfully aware that we may not succeed, that we cannot stop the passing of time, and that one day we will die. Here, again, as far as we can tell, we are the only animals who bear such burdens.

Unlike the other species, we desire to know how the world and our own personal lives will turn out. We can only guess what power in our brain generates such interest. But if anything is clear, it's that this desire sets in perspective the random events that make up our lives and gives those events meaning. This longing also motivates us to design our own futures the best we can. What we think of our potential changes us; today's thoughts affect what kind of persons we become tomorrow. As far as we can tell, none of the other species asks why they are here, where they came from, what they are, what the future might hold for them, or how they can improve themselves and the world.

Another major difference has to do with a recent, fascinating finding that neuroscientists call *mirror neuron circuitry.* The structures within each human brain form a unity, involving about 100 billion neurons, as well as trillions of support cells called *glia*. The term *mirror neurons* identifies a scattering of brain cells that fire when we move or see others move. They seem to be the source of our ability to copy the physical actions of others, by observing them. Because of today's availability of video, which can be viewed over and over again, a child who is reasonably well coordinated, and whose mirror neurons are healthy, can watch professional golfers on tape, and then take in hand a suitably sized club and immediately put a good swing on a ball, copying the pros. In the days before readily available film, the young took a long time to pick up the game.

Scientists have found that healthy mirror neurons also enable us to make out, instantaneously, from the facial expressions, gestures, and body language of others, what they are feeling and what their intentions toward us are at given moments. We recognize whether they are congenial, indifferent, or hostile. The neurons tell us to flee or fight when threatened and to relax and bond with those who smile and welcome us. They also may have something to do with our ability to empathize when we see pain in others. Scientists have found that these neurons in autistic children are damaged, weak, or otherwise unhealthy, a discovery that helps us understand why they have difficulty relating to others.

Neuroscientists do find inklings of these capacities in some other animals. They tell us that monkeys, probably apes, and possibly elephants, dolphins, and dogs have undeveloped mirror neurons. But in us they are so numerous and full-blown, they enable us to carry out sophisticated, subtle imitations (Google "mirror neuron circuitry").

We do sex differently; we give it more attention and bring more to the sexual encounter than the other species. Unlike them, we can copulate at almost any time, week-in and week-out, for three-quarters of a century, and increasing numbers of us apparently are bent on trying to do exactly that.

If you engage in sex of any kind with another person, it's important to see that it is primitively *animalistic*. Men have the same testosterone-driven mating urges as do other primate males, and most women have the same urge to bear children and nest as the other female primates.

The other primates' reproductive systems are similar to ours, physically involving in sex the male penis and female vagina.

It looks like we are the only animal that at times pursues sex simply for pleasure (aside from, perhaps, the dolphins in a limited way). Only humans engage in protracted mental and physical foreplay to intensify our pleasure as we build toward the ecstatic explosions of orgasm. We utilize various bodily positions, erotic music, artificial visual stimulation, so-called aphrodisiacs, testosterone boosters, mineral supplements, lubricants, drugs such as Viagra, sex toys, and even mechanical penile implants—all to help us, male and female, get the most out of "doing it."

When couples anticipate marriage, the institution society has seen suited for creating and sustaining family, most pair off for months, if not longer, for what we call courtship. This period often involves blinding attraction, intoxicating euphoria, and intense sexual exploration. Because it leads to a new life of serious and prolonged responsibility, courtship also can be marked by ambivalence and anxiety. Many animals take part in some kind of mating dance, but even the primates closest to us go through nothing like what we do.

Perhaps the most important characteristic of human sex is that we engage in it to know another person intimately and be known in return. For this to happen, real lovers, with deep respect, agree to treat each other as erotic objects. They become naked and make themselves fragile before each other, leaving themselves open to ridicule, rejection, and abuse by the other, risking their own mental and emotional survival. This mutual granting of freedom honors both animal-like attraction and loving commitment. It's the commitment part that turns having sex into *making love,* the authentic intimate act we find so powerful, beautiful, and worth celebrating.

When both love and sex overtake lovers at the same time, they create a sense of wonder, of mystery and of reverence. Yes, the couple also may be driven by *eros;* that is, they may be hot on the trail of tension release, the sheer pleasure of orgasms or the high purpose of producing offspring, all of which are human and can be exciting and gratifying. But if they seek a relationship at a richer, deeper level, they must choose to be vulnerable to each other physically, emotionally, and spiritually during sex, with the intent of each to enrich and pleasure the other.

That we humans engage in intercourse face to face, eye to eye, helps us to infuse sex with more meaning than simply relieving sexual tension, gaining sensual pleasure or producing offspring. In making love in this way it helps us achieve an intimate bonding, a mutual sense of oneness, a spiritual unity. It puts us deeply in touch with the one to whom we want to show special love and with whom we think we can be safe, at peace and complete.

Does any animal besides us give the slightest consideration to *making love* when having sex, making it a spiritual engagement? None that we know of. For two humans to make passionate love stands in stark contrast to the animals' mechanical, loveless way of male-mounting-female for sex. Evolution does not account for the glory of love-making and its special intimacy. Without that intimacy we find ourselves short of spiritual depth in our most intimate of relations.

Morality also sets us apart from the other species. We humans find ourselves governed by moral law that determines whether behavior is right or wrong. Holmes Rolston III notes, "Animals are unable to address the problems posed by morality ... but they do interact in their societies and have their behavioral rules, which must be where ethics got launched." Ethics stand on the most basic conviction that every human possesses inherent worth that we must respect. We inevitably suffer when that worth is ignored or violated. As moral agents, we know we are at our best when we override our basic animal instinct simply to preserve ourselves, and we stand up for everyone's rights, not just our own or those of our offspring.

This moral sense compels us to sacrifice for all humankind and the planet, even if we won't be around for payday. In its highest form, it requires us to respect even our sworn enemies. Do we know of any other species whose members think of such a thing? Other animals clearly show affection to their mates and offspring, and even to us—pet puppies come to mind. Does any species other than *Homo sapiens* consider for a moment what it would mean to care about their enemies? As far as we can tell, only we humans find ourselves under such a moral order.

Societies create different moral codes, but they all work from the same inborn *judicial sentiment*, a judgmental sense that insists on fair play. All humans—any color and culture, male and female, young and old, weak and strong—judge as immoral any unfair actions by anyone, including themselves ("I'm sorry. I was wrong to do that!"). If you observe children as young as eighteen months, too young to have been taught about fair play, you will see them appeal to this judicial sentiment and immediately rant and rave in judgment of their parents and older siblings for the slightest misplaced favoritism or mistreatment.

In this vein, we judge the unfair actions of organizations, corporations and governments, even if what they do doesn't affect us. It's the power of this law, *strangely written on the human heart,* that makes sure no culture survives for long that encourages its strong to murder its weak or its men to rape its women, or that tolerates torture or the selling of children into the sex-slave market.

No, to our shame we humans don't always abide by this moral law. We abuse almost everything we get our hands on, including, at times, those we say we love. But in our right mind, we insist that no one is above this moral law, and we hold everyone accountable to it.

In checking how we stack up against other species, we also note that we are the only animal that intentionally reaches out with respect to others. We give money to save the whales, but neither the whales, nor any of the other endangered species, show the slightest interest in saving us. And as far as we can tell, we are the only species some members of which actually care about leaving the earth better than they found it. We don't blame the other animals for their disinterest, for we get the impression they possess no sense of the future or of right and wrong.

Also, we humans form groups that take time to pay homage to the mysteries of our existence. We try to answer the *why* questions and to fill the profound meaninglessness that afflicts human consciousness. Religious believers organize to offer praise to a personal God who is either "up there," or "in their hearts." No other animal to our knowledge organizes to worship anything.

It's true that we don't all worship in the formal, religious sense. So I am not talking about a *Sensus divinitatis* (a "sense of divinity" implanted in us by God), which is often offered, without evidence, for the existence of God. But even those who aren't religious invariably adore, trust, and give uncritical loyalty to something: riches, knowledge, art, reason, science, mathematics, the military, sex, drugs, or some combination of these. If nothing more, they may feel compelled to stand back in awe before the universe's incomprehensible size, mystery, and beauty, and engage in reverence before *The All*. Whatever they worship, they ask no less of it than religious people ask of God—they expect it to please, protect and prosper them; hopefully, do to all three.

It is we humans who also know we have been sentenced to die. So we think in terms of limited lifespan, of an ending to our being. If we have not lived a reasonable lifespan and life has been good to us, the thought of life ending, and our no longer being, can breed a dread deep inside most of us that we try to ignore and cover. When young, we are haunted by the thought of life coming to an early end. If something threatens to take our life prematurely from us, and we can't do anything about it, we may weep, grovel or rage, or do all of these. We also may wonder whether anything exists for us beyond this life. But whether we die early or late, and whether we've settled in our own minds the question of life after death, when it comes time to die, if our brain is intact and healthy we want to know we've lived our best lives and contributed something to future generations—especially to any offspring we might have. That's a desire of spirit. No other being seems to care one bit about this.

We may curse the contradictions of our existence, but almost all of us appreciate jokes they make possible. We may blush or be angry about our own mistakes, but we also can see the humor in them and chuckle. Does any other creature respond to the irony of its mortal existence in these ways? Not that I've heard—not even the laughing hyena.

Our radical differences from the other animals make us feel superior to them. They also produce strange problems for us. First, they put us out of sorts with our nature. We do not like thinking of ourselves as part of the animal kingdom and have a natural tendency to oppose our natural tendencies. As far as we can tell, no other creatures have trouble owning up to their *animality*. Check this off as one last sign that we are different in kind.

Second, when we cherish too much being *superior* to the other species, we create problems for them, and for ourselves. It's clear that the skeletal frames, flesh and blood, sexual energy, and the instincts we share with the other animals brand us as their kin. For that reason alone, our moral sense calls us to refrain from needless cruelty to them and to find the best possible ways to meet our mutual needs. We don't always do that. We all know of the sad realities of cock and bull fighting, dog and horse racing, animal cloning, circuses, rodeos, animal parks, factory farms, using laboratory animals to test toxic compounds, and the breeding and often brutal killing of animals for sport, furs, and food. When our needs are in unresolvable conflict with those of other animals, however, we must place a higher premium on human life. Yes, we are animals, but our unique spirituality and the powers of meaning, justice and *agapaic* love can prompt and free us to rise above our natural fears and be as much a benefit as possible to all creation.

If this analysis of our distinctiveness doesn't click with you, imagine watching a breaking television news report of a house fire by an on-the-spot, mobile camera unit. The fire began in their kitchen and now is engulfing the whole building. You witness paramedics treating a man and woman for smoke inhalation on their front lawn. You also see that the couple is hysterical, screaming and frantically pointing at the house. The fire has trapped on the second floor their six-year old daughter, Jennifer, and her beloved kitten, Maggie. Two firemen get the picture and plunge into the burning building at risk to their own lives. Will anyone question which subject the men must seek to save first, Jennifer or Maggie? If in their heroism the men safely rescue only Jennifer from certain death, when the parents realize that Maggie has perished, will it diminish their gratitude to the firemen? And would we not be morally outraged if they let the young girl perish while looking for her cat?

Our rage would not arise from some vague interest in having our species perpetuated, but because we cannot remain human and fail to respect that little girl and her family, persons we don't even know. We care for them from the conviction that we humans have become more than *mere* animals and must honor the dignity and spiritual dimensions of our humanity.

We are the only species that …

… engages in incredibly complex mental activities

… invents sophisticated technological tools

… recognizes ourselves as individuals in community

… senses meaning, or purpose, in history and our lives

… tells stories to understand what human life means

… feels compelled to leave the world a better place

… makes intimate love while having sex

… answers to a sense of moral order based on fair play

… possesses a sense of future, of lifetime and of death

… worships one thing or another

… understands and can laugh at the irony of its existence

… finds itself out-of-sorts with its animal nature.

The Chicken or the Egg

These distinctive human features immediately raise a couple of questions we should note: First, what power or powers made us spiritually unique? We have a few answers from which to choose:

1. **God.** Western religions offer their premise that God in heaven made us this way to be His children. We are created *imago Dei*, in the image of an intelligent, creative, moral, supernatural Deity. No scriptures or theologians or ecclesiastical authorities offer solid evidence for such an answer; they simply point to the fact that we are different and can recognize our differences. Without some kind of evidence, secularists won't tolerate resorting to the supernatural.

2. **Biological and cultural evolution.** Scientists say that biological evolution is unpredictable and our extraordinary brain probably results from an evolutionary accident. Species survive by adapting to their environments. Eons ago, our predecessors went through untold number of adaptations, and at some point our mind/brain emerged. Then, through the impact of cultural evolution,

we relatively recently have been brought to the incredibly sophisticated and unique consciousness we have today. Scientists do not address why we humans are here or why we are so different, except to say that the two evolutionary processes—biological and cultural—obviously did a job on us.

3. **Another Power.** Some thinkers believe strongly in purpose for human history and our lives, but they are caught between supernatural religion and science. They cannot accept the ancient idea of a supernatural Creator "up there." But while they affirm evolution, they also cannot see our distinctive consciousness as a biological accident or the product of impersonal atoms. They look, therefore, for other ways to explain what might have caused our human uniqueness.

In this third view, two early twentieth century Frenchmen stand out. The first is philosopher Henri Bergson, who writes of *Creative Evolution*. This evolution is motivated by an *elan vital*, or a vital impetus, a life force or spiritual power, which he identifies with humanity's natural, creative impulse.

Second is the French philosopher, paleontologist, geologist, and Jesuit priest, Pierre Teilhard de Chardin. He conceived the idea of the *Omega Point*, a maximum level of complex consciousness towards which he believed the universe was evolving. (Google these writers for more.)

We'll look further, in later chapters, at the struggle for an alternative to God and evolution. Keep in mind that scientists affirm evolution and demand evidence for any notion that smells of the supernatural or draws on anything but the material brain to explain our uniqueness. Some of them consider Bergson and Tiehard de Chardin *passe*.

A second question is raised by all this talk about what brought us to spiritual consciousness. It's the old one about the "chicken or the egg": Are we conspicuously different because we are spiritual, or are we spiritual because of our special features? In other words, which came first to trigger the other? Here, we hear two different answers that seem to agree.

1. **Biblical religion** says we first were created physical beings (somewhat like the animals), but then God capped His creation by breathing into us the "breath of life" (Genesis 2:7). He didn't do this to the animals, just to our first parents. Bible believers take this to mean that *God's breath,* or Spirit, is what makes us spiritual and unique.

2. **Science** says we always have been animals and our biological brain evolved, with the increasing help of cultural evolution. It did so to the point we could change dramatically and become the animal whose distinctive marks I have reviewed. Whether they see mind and brain as separate or as one and the same, they conclude it is the evolution of our brain that gave birth to our remarkable nature.

Each view says we began as physical beings like animals, but the two differ about how and why we humans came to our special consciousness and nature. I am among those who contend that spirit and our unique nature are interrelated, but I don't know how. Furthermore, from a practical perspective, I don't care.

Three Powers That Define Our Humanity

What is important and clear to me is that, in addition to our *Homo sapiens*, bipedal, big-brain physical features, there are three spiritual powers, or forces, that give significant purpose to being human. The first is the moral imperative I talked about when identifying our distinctiveness. This power tells us deep down that to be whole, we must be both moral and ethical. This means we must be able to look in the mirror and like what we see because we are responding with appropriate respect to the demands of our personal relationships and also doing our best at living virtuously in a complex, interactive world. It involves not only not doing what is wrong but also doing what we know to be right. I suggest that, in the end, almost all the great human issues are ethical.

A second defining force is our irresistible impulse to grasp the meaning, or purpose, of human life, and of our lives. Each of us asks, consciously or unconsciously: "Is there any real purpose to our existence?" At least four different worldview answers emerge from our culture:

1. **Western religion** answers Yes. It insists human existence and our individual lives do have meaning by our status as Children of God. Your purpose is to worship, love, obey, and serve God, and in those actions you will find your particular calling, or meaning.

2. **Nihilism** claims that life has no meaning and is absurd. We are born, we live, we die. That's it. The life instinct, shared by the other animals, asks you to survive and pro-create. Do what you want to do. Other than that, forget about purpose.

3. **Existentialism** says, with nihilism, that we have no evidence of human purpose; but to live without it is too dreadful to think about. We all, therefore, owe it to our-selves to *create* worthwhile purpose for our lives—your life will mean what you make it mean. If you create pur-pose for your life, then you do well to live passionately in accord with it.

4. **Humanism** contends, with no reference to God, that human life does have meaning. It holds that we owe it to ourselves to recognize both this common meaning and the particular purpose of our lives. We also must discover what the two require of us and follow their dic-tates.

I resonate with this humanistic view. I see several areas of human meaning so self-evident that I don't understand how nihilists and existentialists miss them. I am aware that the Bible speaks of some of the same notions about human purpose that I affirm; but I hold them not because the Bible does, but because I have checked them against the voices of history and tested them against my own experience, and I cannot dismiss their significance. See if these points of purpose make sense to you.

First, our purpose is to be in tune with our own dynamic nature, which means we are to grow up. We are developing, evolving creatures. To be whole, therefore, we must not remain children physically, socially, emotionally, mentally, psychologically, or spiritually. If we thoughtfully mature as we move through life's passages and grow old gracefully, we enrich our inner selves. I couch maturity in terms of being authentically who we are, being real persons, being both fully secular and fully spiritual.

Second, at the macro level, we find meaning in helping make "human life more human" for those we touch, for those beyond our immediate reach but whose lives we impact, for our societies, and, not the least important, for ourselves. It enriches us to give something back to the world to help our species thrive and survive. Down through history multitudes have lived shortened, unfulfilled, noncontributing lives. They have suffered disease, impoverishment, starvation, political oppression, wars, and other brutal misfortunes, with little sense of meaning to dignify their existence. I speak of a massive, tragic human sadness that continues today and that you and I cannot erase. At the same time, if you are healthy, have taken care of your needs for shelter, food, clothing, and transportation, and you are able to read this page, you can contribute—in your own small way—to a more just, peaceful, and humane world. The more you try to do that in touch with what is real, the more you enrich others and yourself.

Third, we give powerful meaning to our lives when we identify our skills, find the right kind of work to do, learn how to be our best possible selves, and then figure out how to achieve our goals. We owe it to ourselves not only to use our work to make a living but also to have our lives stand for something worthwhile and honorable; we are enriched when we know we are contributing to the better world I've been talking about. Our world refers to this as *vocation*, or calling. Secular vocational counselors, who will help you work with your gifts, skills, and interests, insist that if you do not find out who you are and pursue your personal *calling*, you will be on the wrong track and never feel your life has had the satisfying meaning it might have had. Discovering and doing what you are *called* to do in your time and place have the power to help you feel whole, whether you commit to it early or later in life.

Fourth, and not least, we fulfill human purpose when we relate both honestly and graciously with family, friends, coworkers, and our other communities. We are so constructed that facets of our personalities only can be fulfilled in such relationships. We cannot be fully human if we live isolated from others. The more you build relationships based on the light of truth and the warmth of an accepting, respectful love, the more you will feel whole.

This last purpose leads us to the second profound power that defines our humanity. I am talking about the love the ancient Greeks called, *agape (Ah-**gah**-pay)*. This special love was directing human life when they and the early Hebrews were struggling to understand what it means to be human, and it is they who called its profound significance to the attention of us Westerners. I suggest that this kind of love forms the basis for spiritual experience that is earthy, secular and substantive, not fluffy, or ethereal. We may or may not benefit if we could be certain as to why and how we became unique among the animals. But to achieve such certainty is not the primary human goal. That goal is to recognize what this love means and requires of us, and then to live by it.

In my book *Create Your Best Life*, I spend ten pages elaborating on *agape*. Here's a three-paragraph summary of that description:

> *Agape* is the perfect love, the only power worth total trust and uncritical loyalty. Being perfect, you can't criticize it, improve it, or ask anything more of it than what it offers. It stands on the notion that we all are connected and dignified by our distinct human features and our spirituality.
>
> *Agape* is not a feeling but is something you do, a practice; it is the way you treat everyone—even the unlovable—with respect, understanding and compassion. It involves extending favor

that *isn't* deserved (grace), and withholding punishment that *is* deserved (mercy).

Agape generates genuine intimacy, because, with its unqualified acceptance, it frees you to let down your defenses and be known. It promotes good health and healing in those who both give and receive it. When you express this love to others, it may trigger similar responses in them to your benefit as well as theirs. Unlike *brotherly love* and *erotic love*, both of which also can be enriching, *agapaic love* can stay alive and enrich you even when it is not returned. How you practice it--either when unprompted or in response to those who express it to you-- determines to what degree you will be a whole human being.

More than just the power to invigorate and direct you and me, *agape* forms the foundation of a worldview we so desperately need in order to survive and thrive as persons, as a nation and as a species. In this day, when the raging notion that only the fittest have the right to survive threatens to demean and destroy us, *agape* alone builds the respect, understanding and compassion that can save us. In the end, *agape* and this book call you to throw your weight behind others of good will and spiritual sense, to honor the best interests of the human family, and of yourself.

To ask the questions about our distinctiveness and spirituality involves us in developing our personal worldviews, or philosophies of life. As rational animals, it is incumbent upon us to fashion them so they pass the two classic tests for truth:

1. **Internal consistency.** This means we do not affirm something on one page ("God exists") and deny it on the next ("There is no God");
2. **External correspondence to what is real.** This means we avoid superstition, timeworn tradition, nonsense, and wishful thinking (all of these are bad). It asks us to affirm whatever fits the facts as to what is important and how we can best live.

When your worldview is internally consistent and reflects the real world, it helps ground, integrate, balance, and liberate you—it supports your goal to be whole.

This leads us to the important question we'll explore in the next chapter: How do you develop a worldview built on reality?

Philosophy asks the simple question: What is it all about?
Ralph Waldo Emerson

It is a great advantage for a system of philosophy to be essentially true.
George Santayana

Is it given men to judge the truths, to decide the fate of the truths? On the contrary, it is the truths which judge men and decide their fate and not men who rule over the truths.
Lev Shestov

America is the only country where a significant proportion of the population believes that professional wrestling is real but the moon-landing was faked.
David Letterman

CHAPTER 3:

YOUR TAKE ON THINGS

Human Questions

You start out as a secular creature with little if any spiritual awareness. Like all mammals, you begin by sucking at your mother's breasts. You soon awaken to your fingers and genitalia and to adults who feed and burp you and clean up your messes. But one day, your brain develops to the point that life becomes more than body parts, food, and sensual gratification. Your *inner eyes* of self-awareness open, and you see yourself as an individual being, even as you know you also are part of a family and of the larger human enterprise. As you mature, this awareness and tension deepen, and you increasingly realize that you do best not only to express your basic animal desires but also to transcend them, to live with worthwhile purpose and to have your most noble thoughts direct your behavior. I see this as spiritual development.

This awareness may start when you are first smitten by your parents' love or terrorized by their rejection, when you first hear of a loving or a judgmental God, when a sibling is born or someone close to you dies, or when you initially become aware of the *human condition*, marked by evil and mass suffering in the world. But no matter what awakens it in you, you begin to ask, and then consciously or unconsciously wrestle with, questions of meaning that have spiritual implications:

Why is there what is, rather than nothing?
Where am I, and what am I supposed to do?
What is a lifetime, and why should I try to live it?
Why is the world a mess and how do I get through it?

How can I know whether someone's worldview is true?
What can I contribute to the quality of life around me?
How are my brain and my consciousness connected?
What will my love for myself and others mean to me?
What, if anything, is ultimately real, or true?
To whom or to what am I finally responsible?
What is going to happen to me when I die?
What am I to make of all the nonstop talk about God?

Every time we ask such questions, we mark ourselves as meaning-seeking creatures of spiritual curiosity. Simply by asking, we take our place in that marvelous, age-old, strictly human endeavor to understand ourselves and the physical, social and spiritual contexts of our lives. I suggest that *asking* by itself is a spiritual exercise. But if we find evidence-based answers that help connect us to what is real, to the human family, to those closest to us, and to worthwhile purpose for our lives, they may bring both *warmth* and *light* to our search for what it means to be fully human.

For the past century and a half or so, the remarkable findings of cutting-edge scientists have been invalidating traditional answers to these questions, answers we had either inherited or found for ourselves and adopted. Thus, if you and I are to live with integrity today, we must know something about these findings. In this book I cannot cover all of the new knowledge and all of the nuanced arguments both scientists and their critics make, but I can introduce some of them, which I'll do, so you will get the idea.

Once we begin searching for answers to the great questions, we leave childhood innocence behind and relate differently to everything and everyone who matters to us. In the same way as with our sexual energies, we cannot for long ignore our spiritual yearnings without blocking our search for fulfillment.

The question this book urges you to answer for yourself is: "What will it take for me to be fully secular and fully spiritual?" I've designed the discussions ahead to help you answer this question. If you have been sentimental in affirming the spiritual, what you read will help you understand what it means to be rational, worldly-wise, and self-critical. If you've been a hard-nose secularist, hesitant to trust any claims about spirit, this book will challenge you to be more open-minded without being gullible. If you've been unable to bring the spiritual and secular together in some measure of realistic balance, what you find here should help you find a more solid equilibrium.

Religion as an Understandable Starting Point

From the beginning of human time, religions have sought to point the way for people through the darkness of the world. Throughout history, religious leaders, by their observations and uncomplicated, experiential tests, have helped create a vocabulary to explore the universe's mysteries. They also have enabled people to organize their ways of responding to the human predicament (we'll get to this predicament shortly). People always have been drawn to religion in search of not only spiritual guidance but also tribal identity, supportive community, ritual, mystical ecstasy, ethical structure, a sense of place in the larger scheme of things, and comfort in dealing with death.

In the years before sophisticated scientific knowledge, leaders of religions concluded universally that the mysterious material world derives from, and is governed by, a supernatural force, or forces, greater than itself. To identify this nonmaterial power, different cultures have spoken of the Spirit of God, the Holy Spirit, the Great Spirit, the Higher Spirit, the Higher Power, or the Great Nameless Power. Many personalized this force and made it into a deity. Between East and West, researchers have cataloged over 2,500 distinct gods and goddesses.

Researchers today identify seven world religions that continue to influence major blocks of the human family: Buddhism, Christianity, Confucianism, Hinduism, Islam, Judaism, and Taoism. With some overlap, each has its distinctive worldview, which it sees as the *Truth* and the true source of spiritual depth. They all have spawned a variety of schools of thought and many sects, all of which compete with one another and with other cults, and tribal and state religions.

Purists among Western secularists scorn the supernatural gods of religion as figments of imagination and wishful thinking. These secularists are atheists, or anti-theists. In light of current scientific knowledge, they see all beliefs in the supernatural and spiritual as ridiculous. Gods exist, they say, because human beings think they need them; and most make them in their own image. These materialists, however, must forge their own worldviews on the anvil of religion's influence—they cannot ignore Roman Catholic dogma and Protestant teachings that permeate our culture. They must do battle with the hard fact that belief has not died but embedded itself deeply in our national consciousness. Author Salman Rushdie says with irony, and a wry smile: "We atheists are as occupied with God as are religious people."

Whether religious or not, if you want to be a whole person, or authentically spiritual, you do well to have some grasp of what the dominant religions say and let them help you clarify your own take on things. But the task is not easy and your choice is not as simple as either/or.

Finding Out Where You Stand

I invite you now to look briefly at twenty historic belief systems that continue to present themselves. Reviewing them can help you surface any changes you might want to make in your own worldview as you explore what being secular and spiritual means. Using Internet search tools, you can explore these systems for a broader, deeper picture than what I offer here, and one day you may want to pursue any or all of them in more depth. For now, I encourage you to scan these thumbnail sketches, asking of each: "Where does my worldview stand in relation to this one?"

> **Animism:** Spirits dwell in all manifestations of nature, such as springs, streams, trees, and mountains. When the volcano explodes, believers view the spewing lava, smoke, and noise as signs that the spirits are angry.
>
> **Idolism** (Idolatry): Statues, icons, pictures and images can harbor spiritual powers worthy of adoration. Nonreligious and religious people often make *idols* of their parents, national heroes, and sports and entertainment stars.

Paganism: The natural life force—not a supernatural God—deserves respect. The force's expressions are often seen as the work of goddesses and gods. Pagans focus ethically on living by a responsible freedom.

Pantheism: God is everything, and we, with everything else, are a part of God. The stars, bacteria, goldfish, mountains, mosquitoes, flowers, fire, water, and golden retrievers—everything is and shows forth God

Panentheism: God is the universe's animating force, including universal morality. Everything is *in* God, but it doesn't exhaust God's reality. God is the spirit within us, nurturing us and calling out the best in us.

Deism: An unimaginable, creative power long ago brought the universe and us into being but is no more involved in our lives than are watchmakers in the operation of the timepieces they've assembled.

Polytheism: A number of limited gods and goddesses are deemed important spiritual powers in nature (fertility, the sun, rain), and in human emotion, experience and aspiration (sex, war, peace).

Stoicism: Laws of the material universe control us. To be happy, we must adapt to them and to the particular lot in life into which we have been cast, and adaptation may include sincerely loving those who share our destiny.

Theism: One supernatural all-knowing, all-powerful, everywhere present, loving God created and governs everything. The Hebrew-Christian-Islamic theistic belief systems have dominated many cultures of the world.

Mysticism: We cannot know what is ultimately real, but certain dedicated people, in states of spiritual ecstasy, may grasp truths inaccessible to the rest of us and may experience an ecstatic spiritual union with God.

Gnosticism: The physical world created by God imprisons the divine in us. Special people find the god within and know secrets that others don't. This notion flourished and rivaled Christianity in its earliest centuries.

Satanism: A profane (*against the temple*) reaction to religion that urges the worship of the devil and what most people consider evil. Its rituals burlesque and blaspheme the God of the three major theistic religions.

Hedonism: Pleasure is the good (or god). Theaters, stadiums, art galleries, resorts, spas and sex clubs are hedonist's sanctuaries; eating, drinking, and partying are their sacraments. Intellectual hedonists love learning.

Spiritualism: A spirit world coexists with the material world. When we die, we move to the spirit world to progress toward God. Mediums can put us in touch with the dead to comfort us and help us develop spiritually.

Existentialism: Western deity-myths failed, rendering the world godless, valueless, absurd, and dreadful. A sense of personal responsibility and freedom forces us to make for ourselves any meaning we give to our lives.

Atheism: Theism's failure to 1) provide concrete evidence that an all-powerful God of love exists, and 2) motivate believers to respond to the immense human suffering on this earth, justifies disbelief in God.

Agnosticism: No one knows for certain about a God or a spirit world or any afterlife. We all must remain open, however, even while unconvinced. It's akin to atheism, though a softer, more humble form of rationalism.

Humanism: We must move beyond religions' supernaturalism and the afterlife to knowledge, reason, science and democracy, for the highest good is the integrity, security, health, and pleasure of the human family.

Nihilism: Human life offers no knowledge, purpose or meaning, so values, commitments and loyalties are worthless. This cynical, pessimistic and extreme form of existentialism says that all supposed realities are illusory.

Scientism/Materialism: Only the various manifestations of the material exist and are worthy of our trust. True knowledge comes only by repeated testing and the application of reason to sense experience.

Reading this list, you may have stopped several times and said to yourself: "Yes! Of course! Exactly! That's how I see things!" To bring to consciousness your own worldview, go back and circle the titles with which you more or less agree, and draw lines through those with which you hold nothing in common. And if, perchance, you cannot identify with any of these worldviews, think of a word that captures yours, and then write a few lines to describe it. If all of this unsettles you, and you are not ready to identify your philosophy, take a break and read on.

If you circle *Theism*, which many readers will do, know that the deities of Judaism, Christianity, and Islam are going through tough times, and that belief in such popular gods is not as easy as it used to be, at least for those who are informed and thinking, especially among the young. Along with an awareness that science has captured undeniable knowledge of the cosmos that contradicts what these religions have taught about our origins, what follows will suggest another reason why theism's traditional answers are in trouble.

The Significance of the Predicament

We ask big questions about our existence because both we and the world seem off-track—irrationally chaotic, self-defeating, and beset by enormous problems. We are prompted to ask such questions because we are able to imagine a better self and a better world; we see the difference between what we envision and what is. And because we and the world can, and do, change, we'd like to help make both better.

To describe the quagmires in which all of us feel trapped, spiritual thinkers and self-conscious secularists alike expand on the neutral phrase *the human condition* and employ the more provocative term, *the human predicament*. The predicament captures us at two levels: 1) global and 2) intimate. I offer you no gruesome graphics here, but be forewarned, the realities I review at this point present no pretty picture. When done reading this dark stuff, if you want to wallow in these realities, Google "human predicament."

At the macro level, we as a species suffer immense problems that you and I did not create. Moreover, even working together, we can do little or nothing significant to solve them, at least in the immediate present. They include population growth, climate change, and the gross, inequitable distribution of wealth between and within most societies. Also, war, disease, hunger, drudgery, oppression and senseless suffering continue to plague vast portions of the world's population; and, despite education, religion, and technological advances, they still demean us. All the while, we in the first world threaten the survival of our species with weapons of mass destruction, our ongoing dependence on fossil fuels, and our addiction to conspicuous consumption.

Governments seem increasingly unable to deal with these large problems. The power we give to those we elect to political office tends to corrupt a disturbing number of them. Under the spell of this power, they too readily become trapped in dysfunctional systems and policies of their own making. Ignorance, apathy, lack of imagination, unenlightened self-interest, petty distractions, and feelings of being overwhelmed paralyze the best of governments, including ours.

Some observers hold that we are beyond the tipping point of resolving some of these problems. Others believe we are not out of options and point to solutions we might adopt before it is too late. If the latter are wrong, it's possible humankind may make our beautiful planet uninhabitable in the twenty-first century. Not a pretty picture.

Philosophers, scientists, and theologians of all sorts focus on the built-in problems we face as individuals as we try to face life creatively. They offer several *heavy* reasons why our personal existence is best described as a predicament. Here are some of them:

- We stand under the sentence of death. Life itself causes death. Death negates life. The moment we're born we are dying.

- Everything wears out, breaks down, curdles, dries up, rots, rusts, erodes, spoils, corrodes, weakens, self-destructs, or deteriorates, and finally fades away and dies.
- Being trapped in time and space and constrained by physical bodies, bacteria, viruses, crippling diseases, and brain-breakdowns can assault us at any time, even in our early years.
- Earth torments us with cockroaches, poisonous snakes, perfect storms, killer tornadoes, deadly earthquakes and tsunamis.
- We are set apart by races, genders, nationalities, tribes, religions, and political ideologies that demean and break us down by ignorance, fear, false pride, prejudice, and hatred.
- To be noble in the river of life we must swim upstream against a relentless moral current. To do the immoral and unethical takes no effort at all; it's as easy as floating downstream.
- Those who struggle against the current and achieve a worthy moral record have a tendency to become self-righteous and look down on those who don't do as well.
- It seems natural to engage in dysfunctional, one-sided, self-defeating acts, making us our own worst enemy. We regularly fail to do what we ought to do and indulge in behaviors that harm ourselves and others.
- We can't live up to our own or others' expectations of us and, again religion, the behavioral sciences, and the arts seem unable to make a big difference.
- We're in bondage to "the law of unintended consequences." With mocking contradiction, our best-intentioned actions often have negative effects we cannot imagine ahead of time.
- Our sexual urges and thoughts can be so perverse and odious we must hide them even from our loved ones, and

our deception creates false relationships and distance between us and them.

- We see education as a basic solution to many social problems, but learned people can prove immoral, even criminal: educated Americans kept slaves, denied women the vote, used the A-Bomb twice, and waged the Vietnam, Iraq and Afghan wars.

- We are blind to ourselves: tennis players tend to think they're better than they are; marriage counselors mistreat their spouses; and we all believe we're rational, while we make most choices emotionally and then build rationales to justify them.

- People bent on mayhem and mischief require us to rely on fences, walls, locks, metal detectors, burglar alarms, security patrols, watchdogs, police and armed forces, plus juries, judges and prisons; and many of us still don't feel safe.

- No matter our intellect, wealth, social status, or health, the aging process drags us down, and in the end we cannot stop it.

Depressing, no? Not happy thoughts. So what does this mean for us? With no supernatural solution to life, what hope is there? How can we possibly be better persons, give deeper meaning to our lives and survive inside the predicament?

The first thing some of us can do is to acknowledge the predicament and stop pretending life ought to be a piece of cake. Scott Peck begins his book, *The Road Less Traveled*, with three words: "Life is difficult." He contends that if we don't know, or won't accept this fact, we will constantly feel defeated because we will think life should be easy. As we pursue a better world and a sense of spiritual wholeness, it is important for us to *get real*, to be aware that we face negative, counterproductive powers. In this book, we will explore other things you and I can do to live fully in the midst of the predicament.

We all know that Western religions boldly claim that their caring, everywhere present, all-knowing, all-powerful, and all-loving God can protect and rescue you from the predicament both here and now, and in the *hereafter*. They declare that their Gods will save those who trust, obey and serve them. Serious disbelievers argue that this claim, which they believe has captured and numbed the American brain, is a damaging, sentimental, nonscientific fiction, an unrealistic way of looking at our existence. They challenge the proposition that such a God exists and pose a penetrating question that pinpoints what philosophers call, *The Problem of Evil.* Three centuries before Jesus, the renowned Greek philosopher Epicurus tried to reason with those who believed in the ancient gods of Athens:

> *Either your god wants to abolish evil, and cannot; or he can, but does not want to. If he wants to, but cannot, he is impotent. If he can, but does not want to, he is wicked. If God can abolish evil, and God really wants to do it, why is there evil in the world?*

With our understanding of the scope of the predicament today, nonbelievers put it this way to Jews, Christians and Muslims: "Either your God is pitifully inept, or your all-powerful God just doesn't give a damn."

Robert Malthus, an eighteenth century British cleric, tried to justify belief in an all-powerful, loving god, even as he was aware that governments, including his own, readily conquer weaker peoples and enslave or exterminate them, and that tens of thousands of innocent children in this world die every day from hunger. He suggested that such evils persist as a terrible side effect of God's laws, but that those laws have an overall good and worthwhile effect. I find such reasoning as trite as the throw-away line in response to the question of why God would create so many children, then let them suffer and die so tragically: "Apparently God thinks it worth the risk."

The question remains a hard one for Western religions, each of which says that its God is both great and good. We'll explore some of their answers later. First, as background, we look at how ancient Greek philosophy changed the early Church's worldview.

Why do we take the time to do this? Because, though these changes happened a long, long time ago, they continue to shape our American worldview.

PART TWO
VIEWING WHAT WE INHERITED

In their efforts to impose universal worship, men have unsheathed their swords and killed one another. They have invented gods and challenged each other: 'Discard your gods and worship mine or I will destroy both your gods and you!'

Dostoyevsky

Dubito, ergo cogito, ergo sum.
I doubt, therefore I think, therefore I am.

Rene Descartes

When the white missionaries came to Africa they had the Bible and we had the land. They said 'Let us pray.' We closed our eyes. When we opened them we had the Bible and they had the land.

Desmond Tutu

CHAPTER 4:

GREEKS, ROMANS, AND CHRISTENDOM

Jesus Meets Dualism

What follows is a vastly oversimplified yet, I trust, helpful overview of early and medieval Christianity. Forget the details and try to get the basic drift of things. If you find this material difficult, slow down, take it paragraph by paragraph, and let me walk you through it. Don't hesitate to bail out for a moment and Google whatever is throwing you off. And keep in mind that getting this historical perspective will help you decide how you can look at being a real person today.

Go back to the first century of the Christian era. Christianity sprang from Hebrew roots, sparked by Jesus, a maverick prophet, revolutionary teacher, and acclaimed miracle worker seen as having a direct relation to God. He spoke in parables, or riddles, and often said things that are hard for most people to bear. For example, the logical extension of his commandment to have compassion for and to treat everyone with respect, even *your enemies,* stunned and disturbed his closest followers. At the same time, it identified what they knew deep down they needed to do. As hard as he was on them, they came to believe he embodied what the prophets and philosophers had only begun to figure out about *agape.* His teachings and life, dominated by this love, convinced them he had put his finger on what it means to be whole, or true persons, fully secular and fully spiritual.

Jesus impressed the common folk. They suffered poverty, oppression, and feelings of helplessness under the occupying forces of Rome. Many gladly accepted his news that the God of Israel had not abandoned them or the world. He told them God was establishing his kingdom of justice and peace and, by his Spirit, wanted them to participate in transforming the world to that end. His exuberance, courage, and penetrating message painted for them a hopeful future that both called them and freed them to be their best. At the same time, he outraged the religious and political authorities, because his news threatened their control.

For three years, Jesus rumbled around Palestine, making a nuisance of himself and attracting a lot of attention. Roman authorities, who had gotten wind of him early on, finally picked him up in Jerusalem. They ran him through a mock trial, crucified him, and authorized his burial.

Here's where the story gets weird. As the reports go, a couple of days later God raised Jesus from the dead (the Resurrection). Over the next forty days, on several strange occasions, Jesus met with his followers to tell them what they were to do. On the fortieth day, he gave them final instructions and told them God was sending his Holy Spirit to dwell in them for their mission ahead. Then Jesus pushed off the Mount of Olives in Jerusalem and flew up through the clouds to be with God in heaven (the Ascension). Ten days later, during the Jewish feast of Pentecost, the Holy Spirit came down from heaven.

Sometime thereafter, Jesus' followers began gathering weekly on Sunday, the first day of the week and now Resurrection Day. They did so to set themselves apart from Judaism's sabbath (Saturday) and to keep his spirit, his distinct teachings, and his memory alive by word of mouth. Several decades later, some of them began writing *Gospels*, word pictures of what Jesus taught and did, with accounts of his crucifixion, post-Resurrection appearances, and ascension to heaven. They varied their reports so his gospel, or *good news*, could be heard by Jews, Greeks, Romans, and pagans, as well as by his followers, the Church, or his "called-out ones."

The four Gospel writers, whose works the Church chose to put at the beginning of the New Testament, portrayed Jesus as the Promised One of Israel, a spiritual genius, the teacher of teachers, the "visible expression of their invisible God," and the "Authentic Human" for whom the world had been waiting. They saw his life and death in behalf of the world as the certain sign of its eventual coming to the kingdom of justice and peace he talked about. Interestingly, both the Gospel of John and the epistles (letters to the early, newly formed churches), most of which scholars think were written by St. Paul, clearly show influence by the Greek *dualistic* worldview, which we'll review shortly.

Jesus seemed intent on revitalizing the Judaism of his day. He had found it spiritually dead because of stifling rules and regulations, insensitivity to the most vulnerable among them, and a seemingly incurable tribalism. Tribal religion forms, by the way, when believers give unwavering loyalty to their own special deity. Their god exists not only to protect them and serve their interests but also to bless their prejudices by never asking them to outgrow their provincial and defensive small-mindedness. The tribal mindset and worldview, by the way, is a self-invalidating trap into which all religions, philosophies, or political ideologies easily fall and something to which none of us is immune. Jesus' followers, after starting out as a Jewish sect, ended up creating Christianity, a new religion—Jewish at heart, but originally nontribal and strangely open to being shaped by non-Jews.

Monism and Dualism

Several centuries before Jesus, during an era of ferment in the search for human meaning, in both the East and West, the great Greek philosophers, Socrates, Plato, and Aristotle being the three most famous, solidified a worldview based on *metaphysical* (beyond the physical) dualism. In his *Republic, Book VII,* Plato famously illustrates dualism in an allegory. He has Socrates describe to Glaucon (Plato's brother) a group of people chained all their lives in an underground cave, facing a dark wall. The prisoners, who cannot turn their heads, see flickering shadows on the wall ahead of them made by people passing in front of a fire behind them. The prisoners naively take the moving images on the wall to be reality, which, of course, they are not; it's the people moving behind them that are real. According to Socrates, shadows are as close as we get to viewing reality.

This analogy revealed dualism's *two* realms. The first is the physical, illusory, temporary, and imperfect world we experience every day through our five senses.

The second realm is metaphysical; it's made of eternal, perfect, absolute, universal, nonphysical but real *forms* that exist outside our world. These forms give birth to temporal, imperfect, particular expressions of themselves in our material universe. In the same way that Plato's prisoners cannot see the real people walking behind them, we mortals cannot peer into the eternal, perfect realm and see these forms themselves but only imperfect expressions, or reflections of them. For example, we cannot see the eternal, perfect form of *treeness,* because it abides in the metaphysical realm. What we see, smell and touch in the physical realm are particular expressions of that form: oaks, palms, pines, redwoods, and so on.

Jesus, some 400 years after Plato, was not schooled by Greek philosophers. He learned from the Jewish prophets. He picked up their worldview in books bearing their names in the Hebrew Bible, what Christians call the Old Testament. Unlike the Greeks, the prophets were *monists,* that is, they believed not in *two* realms, material and nonmaterial, as did *dualists,* but in the *one* realm they inhabited, the three-deck universe:

Deck 1—the heavens far above, where God and angels abide
Deck 2—the flat middle world here where we live and die
Deck 3—the hot nether region, where Satan conjures up evil

The prophets saw our middle-deck world as real and good but incomplete and caught in the predicament. They viewed themselves as spokespersons for their God, who they said, in a nontribal way, was the universal, true God, the God who plays no favorites but who calls *all* humans to work for peace and justice based on human dignity. Jesus followed in the train of these prophets, affirming this world as real and as the important arena in which Israel's God was conducting his risky, human enterprise based on *agape,* the special love I talked about earlier.

Two centuries before Jesus, the marching armies of the emperor Alexander had spread the Greeks' polytheism and philosophy of dualism all over the Roman Empire. So, when early Christians tried to sell their message of monism to the Greco-Roman world, both a well-established religion and a different philosophical tradition were waiting for them everywhere they went.

The Jew Paul, formerly Saul of Tarsus, was an early persecutor of Christians but underwent a dramatic conversion. He told the world that Jesus had spoken to him through a light from the heavens, and that he had come to see Jesus as God in human flesh, as a god-man among men. Paul went on to found Christian churches throughout the Greco-Roman world made up of Greeks, Romans and Jews. Despite his Jewish background and powerful sense of connection to Jesus, many scholars conclude that his brilliant analytical mind became influenced by philosophical dualism. They often criticize him for not so much teaching the religion *of* Jesus, but a religion *about* Jesus.

In the first three centuries of the Christian era, believers possessed more scriptures than we recognize today, and they developed a variety of traditions. One thing they all secretly agreed upon, however, was that the crucified and living Jesus, not Caesar, was the world's divine ruler; and they generally stood together. During this time, some emperors tolerated Christians. Others saw them as peddling superstition and constituting a threat to the empire, prompting them to persecute the "strange believers" and drive them underground into the famous catacombs.

Early in the fourth century, the Roman emperor Constantine saw a mystical vision of the cross of Jesus in the sky and, like Saul, underwent a dramatic conversion to Christianity. He immediately proclaimed it an "acceptable religion," giving it official status throughout the empire. Before the century ended, church leaders had added 27 writings to the 39 books of the Hebrew Bible, which became their Bible made of two testaments, the Old and the New.

By the fifth century the Greco-Roman gods petered out, and barbarian Goths from the north sacked Rome and laid waste to the empire. The Church, by then well established, found itself in the right place at the right time and with enough of a hold on the masses to fill the political power vacuum created by the empire's collapse.

Christendom in Medieval Conflict

By the sixth century, the form of Christianity historians have labeled *Christendom* emerged with a worldview built on three foundations:

1. **Greek dualism:** God's absolute truth abides in a supernatural, eternal realm,while we live in the natural, temporary world.
2. **Christian doctrine:** The true Creator God sent his Son Jesus to our world from the eternal realm to reveal God's truth, to build his Church, to set up his spiritual kingdom, and to save humankind.
3. **The Roman concept of empire:** The Church's organized all-male hierarchy is the political "power tool" God has chosen to take charge of the world and establish his kingdom.

With a dualistic worldview and a solid institutional base, the Church not only gave structure to an emerging new empire, it also provided the conceptual framework, or worldview, that would hold the mind of Western Europe together for centuries to come. In this tipping-point sixth century, Christendom's God took center stage in the West. To this day Westerners have been unable to avoid the voice of this "Primary Actor" on their understanding of what human life is supposed to be.

In Christendom, influenced greatly by Paul's Epistles, the Hebrew *upper deck* where God abides melded into the eternal realm of Greek dualism. Thus, Church leaders dropped any goal Jesus had to transform our middle-deck world to a realm of justice and peace. They deferred the people's dream of such a world, by creating in them a lust for a *happy life-after-death*. They argued that this life is like a brief puff of smoke, while eternity is forever. Life here, they said, may be filled with suffering and sorrow, but the forever hereafter for the faithful will be nothing but bliss.

All the while, medieval Church theologians had no real knowledge of science. They interpreted nature's mysteries from an ancient, mythological point of view, seeing the middle deck where we live as a veritable "enchanted forest," the home of monsters, witches, giants, and fairies. They held that angels sent by God from above and demons let loose by Satan from below travel here to intervene in human affairs. They told the common folk that these forces can influence their behavior ("the devil made me do it!") and control nature's powers for their benefit ("the earth quaked, and many people died, but my guardian angel protected me!"). They taught them that through prayer the faithful could tap God's power to stave off Satan and make their lives good. They also were told that God blesses faithful people and punishes disbelievers, giving each a foretaste of the final judgment that will send everyone either to heaven or hell. The Church's prime purpose was to scare the hell out of people and the people out of hell. In this second half of the first millennium of the Christian era, the gospel of the Church hierarchy sounded something like this:

> **The Bad News:** God dwells above in heaven, the metaphysical eternal, spiritual realm of perfect beauty, truth and bliss. But you, as a physical being, endure the temporal predicament of this world, marked by suffering, death, doom, and gloom. As a miserable sinner you are unworthy to enter God's realm and should be sent straight to hell.
>
> **The Good News:** You cannot break into God's realm and be acceptable to him by your best efforts or by reason. But in Jesus, God broke into the predicament on your behalf. Fortunately, God has established us as His Church and given us the keys to heaven. Do what we tell you, and we will lead you to Paradise.

Because of the Church's powerful and corrupt leadership, its hatred of Jews, its disregard for people's suffering, its preoccupation with the afterlife, and its insistence on blind faith and obedience to its authority, historians refer to this bleak, medieval period of the sixth through the tenth centuries as *the Dark Ages*.

Then things got worse. In 1065, the Muslim Turks took over Jerusalem and massacred 3,000 Christian pilgrims. Three decades later, Pope Urban II launched hordes of Christian zealots to take revenge and reclaim the holy city, on what historians call *The First Crusade*. It ended in 1099, with the siege of Jerusalem and the heinous slaughter of some 10,000 Muslims and Jews, including women and children. In the twelfth and thirteenth centuries eight other crusades followed.

Toward the end of the twelfth century, Pope Innocent III instituted *the Inquisition*, in which Dominican friars in France set up heresy trials for those in the Church who were suspected of holding, unacceptable beliefs. Those determined to be guilty were tortured and burned at the stake. This dreadful time dragged on, in one form or another, here and there, for the next four centuries.

The Church, like brutal empires before it, used its menacing power to subjugate the masses. Its worldview was unchallenged in Western Europe through the twelfth century. Rather than being one option among many, it was the one and only way everyone looked at reality—they all believed in Jesus and God, in heaven and hell, and in the power of Church. No one could have imagined not believing.

They also hadn't the faintest idea of what was to happen next.

While we all kneel let one man speak to God thus: 'Take this book back;
we men, such as we now are, are not fit to go in for this sort of thing,
it only makes us unhappy.' This is my proposal, that we beseech Christ
to depart from our borders. This would be an honest and human way
of talking —rather different from the disgusting hypocritical priestly
fudge ...

Soren Kierkegaard

The Sea of Faith
Was once, too, at the full, and round earth's shore
Lay like the folds of a bright girdle furled.
But now I only hear
Its melancholy, long, withdrawing roar,
Retreating, to the breath
Of the night-wind, down the vast edges drear
And naked shingles of the world.

Matthew Arnold

Gott ist tot.

Friedrich Nietzsche

CHAPTER 5:

THE DEMISE OF THE DEITY

Cutting Down the Enchanted Forest

Until the thirteenth century, people in the Western World believed that God inspired Moses and certain ancient Hebrews to tell us fanciful stories—Adam and Eve, Noah and his ark, Jonah and the great fish, and so on. The storytellers sought to explain how we got here, why we are so screwed up, and what we must do to minimize the predicament's damage. They came to their understandings not by observation, experimentation, testing, and reason but through dreams or flashes of mystical insight. It is called *revelation*, as in *revealed by God*.

Under the influence of the Greek philosophers, almost everyone in the West trusted the *deductive* method of reasoning to lead them to truth. This method moves from the acceptance of a *general* premise (humans must eat to survive) to a *particular* conclusion (I am a human; I must, therefore, eat to survive). Through the fourteenth century, no serious, outside challenges had been mounted against the Church's basic premises: "All have sinned against the Creator God and deserve His wrath; God sent his Son, Jesus, to save us from our sin and build his Church to give us this truth; submission to the Church's authority will lead you to Paradise." The Church hierarchy told the common folk to accept these teachings without evidence, that is, on faith: believe them because we say so, and don't ask questions. The people bowed to the Church, because, while they were weak and life was brutally cold and dark, it was strong and made them feel warm and secure in the light of God's truth.

But now, explorers of the physical universe—unconvinced of the Church's take on things, because of what they were discovering—began sowing seeds of distrust in the deductive method as the only way to truth. They realized, too, that if you start with a general premise that is not correct (humans can fly like birds), it leads you not to a particular truth but to a falsehood (I'm human; therefore, I can fly like a bird).

They also began using another way to arrive at truth: the *inductive* method, which we have come to know as the scientific method. In contrast to the deductive method, this way of reasoning moves from *specific* facts, found through observation, objective study, testing, and the review of findings by others, to *general* truths about which we can have only a measure of certainty, but upon which we can rely for all practical purposes. Here's an example I've concocted to illustrate such reasoning:

> *We had thousands of people jump out of trees and flap their arms vigorously. We found not only that gravity is still in effect and that hard ground breaks bones but also that humans, to be sure, cannot fly like birds. From never having seen anyone fly, we long had suspected this was true. Now, not because a priest or philosopher has told us, but because of this reliable method of observing and testing, we are convinced of the general truth: humans cannot fly like birds.*

The Church clung stubbornly to the biblical report of a God-created universe with heaven above and hell below. But a few scientific types were putting two and two together and beginning to criticize the Church's supernatural worldview. In observing the heavens with telescopes, they found it filled with globes, which they observed carefully and came to believe the *general* truth (our earth is not flat but round). These thinkers, doing their work *outside the Church box*, began circulating papers to the common folk. More and more eyes were opening to see that the ancient worldview of Christendom did not fit the universe of which they were becoming increasingly aware. Slowly but surely, more and more Europeans were feeling that the Church had led them not to Paradise but to a prison of ignorance, error, and fear.

In the fourteenth century, despite the Church's hard line against secular aspects of Europe's culture, there arose a new devotion to truth, to art, to education, to the sovereignty of each individual, to the entrepreneurial spirit, to respect for commerce, and in science to an increased reliance on observation. We know this blossoming of secular activity, which would last into the seventeenth century, as the Renaissance. On the heels of its awakening, in the fifteenth century, resistance began to shake the Church's authority; and it found itself powerless to stop what we have come to call the Scientific Revolution.

The Church also suffered internal unrest. Early in the sixteenth century, the German priest Martin Luther and the Swiss lawyer John Calvin, among others, launched public protests against the abuse of Church authority. They hoped to reform the Church to serve people's needs. What they did led to a fracture of the Church that we know as the Protestant Reformation. A number of renegade Protestant churches—among them, the Lutheran, Presbyterian and Anglican—survived and aligned with European secular states. Even as these new churches broke with the Roman Church, they retained its worldview based on supernaturalism and dualism—a Protestant supernatural God is still in his heaven.

On the heels of the Renaissance and Reformation came the Age of Reason, or the Enlightenment. Philosophers now were freely pursuing ideas contrary to Church dogma, Catholic or Protestant. Natural science began gaining respect for unrestricted research and the testing of concrete evidence as a legitimate means for obtaining reliable knowledge and banishing superstition. The still-strong Roman Church declared the inductive method *dangerous*, but scientific knowledge continued to become a strong alternative to its teachings. Even churchmen, such as the sixteenth century Polish astronomer Copernicus ("Earth revolves around the sun!") and his seventeenth century follower, the Italian Galileo Galilei ("Earth is not the center of the universe!") embraced the scientific method and stopped bowing to the Church. Sadly, some who challenged Church authority paid dearly for it.

The Process of Secularization

The secular freethinkers of this time helped jump-start what I referred to earlier as the important *process of secularization.* To arrive at truth you take explanations of the natural world out from under the umbrella of supernatural religion, and you directly engage nature on its own terms. You gather evidence, and you draw natural conclusions for the way things work in the physical universe. As noted earlier, the Church had historically viewed the world as an "enchanted forest" fraught with supernatural powers good and bad. Secular scientists engaged in *disenchantment,* or the process of *secularization.*

This process has affected all of us to one degree or another. Consider a couple of examples that illustrate it. First, imagine you visit Wyoming's Yellowstone Park and come upon Old Faithful. A local native tells you an angel, on a regular schedule, causes the boiling water to blast from the hole in the ground and shoot high in the air. Minutes later the park ranger gives his lecture which includes the geothermal explanation. If you buy what the ranger says, rather than the tale about the angel, you've taken part in *the process of secularization* and are, at least with regard to this matter, *secularized.*

Second, if a neighbor is killed by lightning and you conclude that God punished that person for some kind of sin; you've not begun to *disenchant* the world. If you believe the HIV/AIDS epidemic will be thwarted by prayer rather than by educating people about the virus, distributing condoms, and developing medicines, then secularization hasn't made much of a dent in your consciousness.

I first heard the following story sometime in the 1980s. Stop me (or skip it) if you've already heard it.

A boy comes home from Sunday school and his father asks him what he learned.

Nothing, the boy says, lowering his head.

Well, what did your teacher talk about?, his father asks.

Uh, she ... uh, she told us about Moses leading the Israelites out of Egypt.

The father is curious: *She did, did she? Tell me about it?*

The boy pauses, then finally looks up at his father and replies, *Okay.* Here's the story he tells:

The Pharaoh of Egypt made slaves of the Israelites, the Jews of long ago. One day God tells Moses to go to the Pharaoh and say: Let my people go! Moses does what God wants, and when the Pharaoh refuses, God sends a lot of awful plagues on the Egyptians. After a while, the Pharaoh finally gives in, and Moses leads his people out of Egypt across the desert toward the Promised Land. But the Pharaoh, who decides he's been tricked, sends his army after the Israelites to kill them.

About this time, Moses brings his people to the Red Sea, and they can't figure out how to get across. When his scouts warn them that the Egyptian army is in hot pursuit, they begin shaking in their boots. But Moses pulls out his smart phone and calls his Army Corps of Engineers, bringing up the rear. The corps rushes forward with its big trucks loaded with state-of-the-art construction equipment and quickly builds a long pontoon bridge for the Israelites to walk across, which they do. Just as they reach the other shore, the Egyptian army begins driving its tanks onto the bridge. Moses is prepared: He calls his Air Force, and their dive bombers, at the ready, swoop down, blow the bridge to smithereens and the Egyptian Army drowns in the sea.

The father's mouth drops open. After a few moments of silence, he looks the boy straight in the eye and asks, *Now son, be honest with me. Is that really what your teacher told you in Sunday school this morning?*

Uh, well … gosh … uh, no Daddy, the boy says, *but … but if I told you what she told me, you'd never believe it.*

I doubt that the father looked at it this way, but it's clear the son was participating in the process of secularization.

Go back with me to the seventeenth to nineteenth centuries, when scientists were increasing their challenges to Church claims of the supernatural. Freethinkers demanded that the clergy stop intimidating people in order to sustain their superstitions, and that religion not make claims about the universe and human nature until it had evidence gained by repeated observation and serious testing. Scientific secularists were prying open the door of science to discover more truth about the universe; and more and more Europeans, looking for enlightenment based on reason and science, were flocking through it. What we call *the modern age* was being born.

The Scientific Secularized World

When ships left Europe to cross the Atlantic for the new land early in the seventeenth century, they mainly carried nonconforming Christians fleeing religious persecution. Their stated purpose was to worship God without governmental interference, both a spiritual and secular goal. What many of them did when they arrived here, however, was to set up, rather ironically, their own narrow, sectarian colonies. In those communities, believers found a new sense of religious identity and destiny that invigorated and unified them. At the same time, they drove out anyone who believed differently or not at all. And those who dreamed of a *Christian America,* envisioned it only for those who believed exactly as they did.

But in the last quarter of the eighteenth century, as the new republic was being shaped, the likes of Thomas Jefferson and James Madison made sure its Constitution prohibited state religion and protected both the free exercise and the *nonexercise* of religion. The "wall between church and state," as Jefferson put it, gave a boost to the likes of some believers who'd suffered religious persecution in Europe. It also killed the notion of an official *Christian America,* or state church. Instead, it established a robust, secular democracy, one that ensured the freedom of believers and nonbelievers alike and gave momentum to the process of secularization. In a real sense, it officially shifted responsibility for our salvation, as a nation, from God to us. It is important today not to forget how radical this experiment was and still is. It determined that citizens will be free to pursue any religion they desire, or no religion at all. The new state will be governed by reason and fairness without the dictates of organized religion.

Later in the nineteenth century, the earthshaking thinking of Darwin, Freud, and Karl Marx further moved the educated North American mind away from the supernatural toward a secular consciousness. None of them included in their ideas a God who meddles in human affairs, who controls everything we do, and before whom we all ought to bow down. Before the century closed, advances in industrialization and urbanization also helped spread the scientific way of thinking to the American masses. And a barrage of theoretical and scientific attacks on the Bible and faith opened ths consciousness even wider.

Early in the twentieth century, however, despite our federal government's refusal to establish religion, some states enacted laws supporting Christian principles and practices; and fundamentalist Christians fought bitterly against the teaching of "godless" science. In 1925, a Tennessee legal case known as the Scopes Monkey Trial featured a high school teacher accused of teaching human evolution, a practice that was illegal in that state. The trial publicized the controversy between fundamentalists, who said the word of God took priority over all human knowledge, and modernists, who did not see evolution as inconsistent with their faith. The case was seen as both a theological contest and a trial about whether the controversy between creation and evolution could be taught in public schools. Science won. And, at the same time, with new knowledge about the origin, size, nature, and age of the universe, our universities were making evolution standard fare. It soon became the main staple in our secular, educational pantry.

Up until the 1960s, however, Christianity's imprint on society, particularly in the East and Southeast, could be seen every day among the lives of common folk: laws disallowed businesses to operate on Sunday; in many states one could only buy liquor in state-regulated stores; professional sports were not played on Sunday mornings in competition with church services; and the air was not filled with four-letter words. Even the federal government seemed to violate the "separation of church and state" principle by including the phrase *under God* in the Pledge of Allegiance; stamping *In God We Trust,* on our coins; taking oaths on the Bible at inaugural ceremonies; and employing chaplains for the Senate and House of Representatives. Signs of these practices remain today.

Following World War II, in the last half of the 1940s, masses of religious youth from the Bible Belt streamed into secular universities along with veterans whose way was paved by the GI Bill. Most took science courses and heard for the first time claims that conflicted with what their often less educated and biased Sunday school teachers and nuns had taught them. Many were becoming swayed by scientific thinking, becoming sophisticated and secularized. Even the most devout dropped the idea that lightning, earthquakes, and hurricanes were instruments of punishment wielded by an angry God. Some stopped believing that if you pray sincerely you can count on divine cures for your cold or cancer. By the 1950s, medicine, public education and the science industries were radically reshaping American values, systems, and public policy. And God, longtime friend of the American family, began receiving fewer invitations to Sunday dinner.

By the 1960s, brash scientific secularists had taken charge of America. Many observers concluded that the secularization of the country was approaching completion. The churches that still took God-talk seriously found they were like islands in the rough sea of the future. The country's modern optimistic, secular spirit sustained most Americans' faith in the inevitable march of progress toward a future of prosperity and world peace. God might not be able to solve the world's problems, but science could. Roman Catholics and mainline Protestants increasingly tried to combine, to one degree or another, modern reason with ancient faith. But with one foot in one world and one in another, many of them felt divided and on shaky ground.

God Dies and the Foundations Shake

The 1960s dealt faith a further blow. Playing on the bleak words of the nineteenth century Friedrich Nietzsche, *Gott ist tot*, in blood-red letters on a black cover, *Time Magazine's* April 8, 1966, Easter issue (irony, no?) asked: "Is God Dead?" It was not atheists but theologians who urged the magazine to pose this question. These biblical scholars were embarrassed by the simplistic, sentimental acceptance by common church folk of "the Big Guy in the Sky," who directed human affairs. Atheists always had talked about the *absence of* the *presence* of God (he doesn't exist; he's not here, he's nowhere). But these new observers were speaking more of the haunting *presence of* the *absence of God* (he was here, he used to run things, he's gone, and he's left a void!). The void was like the deafening rural silence you can hear when the crickets suddenly stop chirping at night. It generated the kind of sickening emptiness you feel when someone you love suddenly moves away, or dies. Increasing numbers of Americans were becoming suddenly suspicious that no one was watching over us.

At a deeper level, they lamented the failure of faith to help shape the most critical human issues of the day. *Time* printed an obituary from *motive*, a cutting-edge, Methodist student publication:

> *God, creator of the universe, principal deity of the world's Jews, ultimate reality of Christians, and most eminent of all divinities, died late yesterday during major surgery undertaken to correct a massive, diminishing influence.*

This is what the *Death of God* theology is talking about. It isn't saying people won't be religious anymore. And it doesn't refer to a supposedly immortal God who suddenly ceased to exist, or died as we humans die. It's about the dramatic loss of religion's influence on education, politics, business, law, medicine, sexual ethics, and social policy. Indeed, these losses exposed a poignant contradiction: Leaders in these fields may believe personally in a God that lives in the heavens or in their hearts, but their devout faith no longer has the power to dictate how things will work in our secular society.

Many traditional Christians felt an awareness of God's death as a punch in the stomach. At the same time, the country's psyche itself suffered repeated inflictions of specific grief. People now in their twenties can remember the dread and sorrow of September 11, 2001. But much older readers suffer that day as an echo of the late 1960s, when the Kennedys and Martin Luther King, Jr. were gunned down, and the nation was forced to face our racial policies and the Vietnam War as disgraceful failures.

Don McLean's 1971 song *American Pie*, a nine-minute melancholy reflection on the 1960s, reminds us of that time of trauma. Interpreters of the piece insist that McLean's symbol-laden lyrics, with their metaphorical refrain: *The day the music died,* mourn the sudden tragic death of his rock-and-roll hero, Buddy Holly. But most also believe he is recalling those devastating assassinations and the dreadful war, and, equally important, laying bare a broader, deeper *theological* grief, wherein the Church's influence and God seem to be gone. Even nonreligious types find significance in these few lines:

> *I went down to the sacred store,*
> *Where I'd heard the music years before;*
> *But the man there said the music wouldn't play.*
> *And in the streets the children screamed,*
> *The lovers cried, and the poets dreamed.*
> *But not a word was spoken,*
> *The church bells all were broken.*
> *And the three men I admired most,*
> > *The Father, Son and Holy Ghost,*
> > *They caught the last train for the coast,*
> > *The day the music died.*

In the 1970s, interpreters said they saw clear reasons why "the music died" and God skipped town: the civil rights revolution, the Vietnam quagmire, the political assassinations, the Holocaust, the advent of the atomic age, the radical sexual revolution, the upsetting changes in Roman Catholicism effected by Vatican II in the early 1960s, the birth of ecumenism and the interfaith movement, religion's inability to address effectively the injustice, poverty, and crime chewing up our cities, and the seemingly unstoppable march of secularization. While the 1960s were a decade of liberation for some, the era also dealt national optimism a shattering blow, and some key observers felt the country was convulsing toward a nervous breakdown. They saw the pain in America's face and declared we had entered the pessimistic *Postmodern Age.*

In the last quarter of the twentieth century, many religious Americans felt orphaned in a world where the certainty of belief—if not God—had died. At the same time, sentimental attachment to the Christian religion held a tight emotional grip on them. Christians fleeing persecution for their beliefs first colonized this country; the various sects had long established places of worship where their members met weekly for spiritual reinforcement and indoctrination on their distinctive beliefs; and they all found passages in God's Holy Bible to justify their existence. But now, a lot of believers lost their balance as if the universe was slipping from underfoot. The clergy lost their authoritative role in society. Mainline Protestant churches went into membership free-fall; older members were dying and they were failing to attract younger ones, starting a slide to the sideline of influence that continues today. Someone at the time compared organized religion to a listing cruise ship: Most festivities continue on its decks, but below the waterline the hull has sprung a leak and passengers aware of it are either jumping overboard or trying desperately to keep the ship afloat by bailing water with little buckets of faith.

In the belly of this social trauma, Christian fundamentalism was challenging new scientific knowledge and offering sinners the absolute certainty of unthinking faith and a final trip to heaven. It soon began, therefore, to flourish and take over Protestantism's center stage. It also didn't take it long to turn its eyes toward political power. Now, in the twenty-first century, it has become known as the zealous "religious right" and widened its political influence through the Tea Party. It's also known for broadcasting a bizarre, apocalyptic end-of-the world scenario from which its faithful are to be rescued and into which the more frightened and desperate are eager to buy. We'll look at this end-time story in the next chapter.

As the country was losing its confidence in mainline religion, it experienced a widespread surge of interest not only in fundamentalism but also in individual spirituality. People yearned for warmth and stability in an increasingly cold and chaotic world. The vague term *spiritual* suddenly became a buzzword: spiritual formation, spiritual music, spiritual intelligence, spiritual discernment, spiritual direction, spiritual practices, spiritual disciplines, spiritual fitness, spiritual retreats, spiritual this and that.

Shortly before the new millennium, respected mythologist Joseph Campbell expounded on the myths of ancient cultures in a popular Bill

Moyers' TV series, creating what someone called "Public Television spirituality." *The New Yorker* featured a cartoon in which two chic young women sipped Merlot at a sidewalk café, with one confessing to the other: "I've felt funny a couple of times, but I can't say I've ever had a real spiritual experience." This fascination with spirituality may have been superficial, but in the new materialistic world, with religion in turmoil, many people were suffering a deep thirst for depth and meaning. All together, the sexual revolution, the drug culture with rock-and-roll, Monday Night Football, and the digital entertainment explosion that led to HDTV, smart phones, wi-fi, and Netflix could not quench that thirst.

Since the 1960s, our American culture has offered a one-sided, secular sense of self. It has given us new gadgets, which are seen as scientific advances, but no larger sense of meaning. With fewer adults exposed to spiritual formation, great art, music, or literature, many seem asleep to the wonders that always have inspired people to be their best.

Many reared in religion have dropped beliefs that once grounded them, because those beliefs didn't hold up outside synagogue or church walls. Most can now tell you what they don't believe but not what they do believe. Sadly, some, rather than believing nothing, now believe anything.

Many young people today dote on the present with little sense of history. Too few can tell you the principles they live by or the big ideas on which they'd stake their lives. No worthy dream pulls them forward, so they don't know where they're going, or why.

Many young and old alike have no realistic framework for thinking, no viable worldview on which to hang their lives. They cannot, therefore, ask profound questions about human meaning, let alone identify viable answers. Lacking a reliable intellectual rudder and moral compass, they narcotize themselves with technology's latest toys, money, drugs, and entertainment, or they plod through their days as if walking uphill in sand. And when their hollow lives fall apart, few find anywhere to turn but to superstitious religion or psychotherapy.

Today's rampant commercialism, ruthless competition, and cynicism exhaust most secularized people who give thought to how their lives can count for something worthwhile. Despite their disillusionment with just about everything, they continue to crave something to believe in beyond mere physical and economic survival. Some of the young still search for energizing patterns of meaning and purpose in the universe, in their nation, in their communities and in their own small lives. If, as someone put it, "the Middle Ages was an era of faith in search of enlightenment," these secularists might make us say: "The twenty-first century in America is an age of enlightenment in search of an authentic faith."

Ask Americans today what they believe is ultimately real or true. The majority, overtly religious or not, automatically answer, *God*. They don't all mean the same thing by *God*. And some are not certain of their answer, but *God* trips easily off their tongues. By contrast, a minority with training in science and no concern for God often say with great certainty that "the material universe and the human brain" are all that are ultimately real for us. Another minority of thinkers simply answers the question with "I don't know." Then, still others combine two or three of these answers in one mix or another, but they don't all give each answer the same weight.

We'll look to a further understanding of the first two answers in the next few chapters.

Extreme and bizarre religious ideas are so commonplace in American history that it is hard to speak of them as fringe at all.

Phillip Jenkins

Religious belief is without reason and without dignity, and its record is near-universally dreadful ... if God existed, and if He cared for humankind, He never would have given us religion.

Martin Amis

Admittedly, I do have several bones--whole war fields full of bones, in fact--to pick with organized religion of whatever stripe. This should be seen as a critique of purely temporal agencies who have, to my mind, erected more obstacles between whatever notion of spirituality and Godhead one subscribes to than they have opened doors.

Alan Moore

CHAPTER 6:

AMERICAN CHRISTIANITY TODAY

The Biblical Story and True Believers

Ultra-Orthodox Jews, pre-Vatican II Roman Catholics, devout Eastern Orthodox believers, Protestant fundamentalists and some evangelicals, and fanatical Muslims, along with the cults that spring from these traditions, all see faith in terms of giving mental assent to dogmas narrowly drawn from simplistic biblical interpretation. Because they already have the truth about God, the universe, human nature, and the significance of history, those who think this way ignore new knowledge from the sciences. They also are more ready to spread their beliefs than pursue truth, or open themselves to dialogue with other believers or nonbelievers.

These "true believers" insist the Bible's view of an enchanted world, in which God, demons, angels and other "spirits" intervene in human affairs, offers an accurate depiction of reality and the foundation for a genuine spirituality. Most of traditional Christians who are estimated at 2 billion worldwide, and Muslims estimated at 1.6 billion, find comfort in the promise of life after death. They say it helps them to deal with the mysteries they find in themselves and in the world, and to fit their lives into the grand scheme of things. They also are slow to exchange the warmth of their faith for the cold universe defined by secular science, no matter how much light it affords.

You probably are familiar with the Bible's creation accounts. They answer for us our first two questions: "Where did everything come from?" and "Why is life such a predicament?" But to make sure we're on the same track, stay with me for a moment while I recount this story, which forms the foundation of the Christian belief system and continues to fill the American atmosphere.

The supernatural God of the ancient Hebrews (Jesus' God and Father, the Muslims' Allah) created in five days, out of nothing, six to ten thousand years ago, the universe, including our sun, moon, stars, and Earth, with its mountains, oceans and the estimated 10-15 million species alive today—all exactly as we find them now.

On the sixth day God created "in His image," two full grown human beings, male and female, innocent and immortal. God made the male first and called him Adam. Out of one of the man's ribs, God formed a female companion for Adam, whom Adam called Eve. Somewhere in the Middle East, God placed them in a garden paradise that He called Eden. The male and female were to praise, live in harmony with, and enjoy God forever. This is how and why we got here.

Weary from all his work, God took the seventh day off to rest.

Right off, as we noted earlier, God instructed the first humans to multiply by having sex, to care for their offspring, and to dominate the Earth and its other creatures. He added one negative, stern warning: "Don't eat fruit from the tree of the knowledge of good and evil or you'll die." Unfortunately, Adam and Eve listened to a talking snake, assumed in later Church teachings to be the fallen angel Lucifer, or the Devil, or Satan, in disguise. The evil serpent told them that if they did eat of the forbidden fruit, they would not die but become like God, knowing the difference between good and evil. You are aware that I am not making this up, and you also know—even if you're not a part of this religious tradition—that Eve picked the forbidden fruit, gave it to Adam, and they both sank their teeth into it.

As the Bible story goes on to tell, God is enraged by the disobedience of the humans he has created. He strips them of their innocence, so they come to know not only good and evil but also shame and guilt. He banishes them from the Garden, assigns the male he has made to hard labor and condemns the woman to pain in childbirth and the rule of her husband. God then extends Adam's and Eve's punishment by having them pass on their sinful nature—their inclination to immorality—to their children, who then pass it on to their children, and on and on through subsequent generations, right down to you and me.

Literal interpreters of the scriptures tell us that this curse is why we suffer the human predicament we looked at earlier, and why it is our destiny to spend eternity separated from God. Our first parents blew it big-time, and, for this, we all have to suffer.

In the West and Middle East, down through the ages this story has sown the seeds not only of guilt and phobia about sin but also of the subjugation of women. Jewish, Christian, and Muslim leaders have employed this myth to justify controlling and humiliating women. They note that God created Eve as an afterthought and an appendage to Adam; that she ate the forbidden fruit first and then seduced Adam into eating; that God punished her by having her husband rule over her; and that it is the first woman's disobedience that led to God's wrath and brought us to death and eternal damnation. Based on this reasoning, male religious authorities have narrowly restricted the behavior of women and inflicted on them second-class status in synagogue, church, and mosque. They have oppressed women by telling them to obey their husbands no matter how they are treated. They have taken from them the fullness of human sexuality by reducing them to "baby factories." (if married, you can do it for reproduction, with your husband on top, and as long as you don't enjoy it too much). As a result, the predicament has been harder on women than on men, and tragically, scandalously so.

Traditional believers take the creation stories as historical accounts, as facts, because they find them in the scriptures they deem to be God's Holy Word. You may think it ridiculous for adults in this scientific age to believe this about the universe and human nature, but some 150 million Americans accept most of it, if not all of it, in just that way.

The first three chapters of Genesis tell us how we got here and why we suffer the predicament. So, what answer do the three major religions give to our third question: "What will it take for me to live my best possible life?" They say that to be our best selves and live our best possible lives, we must "get right with God," learn God's will, obey Him, and follow their prescriptions. If we do that, God will protect us and help us work our way through the predicament. All religions have their own prescriptions for how you get right with God, and they all tell you theirs is the right way.

In ancient Judaism, priests on their temple altars sacrificed animals (bulls, lambs, doves, and the like) to *cover* the sins of the people so they could be pleasing to God. God reportedly told Moses that since "the life of the flesh is in the blood" (Leviticus 17:11) blood must be shed to cover, or wash away the people's sin and pacify God's wrath. So, for a couple of thousand years before Jesus, the priests regularly, in ritualistic sacrifice, spilled the blood of animals the people brought to them.

When the Romans destroyed the Jewish temple in Jerusalem in 70 AD, the Pharisees, a major political power in Judaism and predecessors to the tradition of rabbis, talked the other Jewish officials into putting an end to both the priesthood and animal sacrifices. They then shifted worship from the temple altar to the synagogue, where to learn, interpret the ancient laws, and observe tradition were seen as God's order of the day.

Christianity was in its formative stage when the Jews stopped sacrificing animals. Ironically, the earliest Jewish followers of Jesus, including the Gospel writers, saw his crucifixion in light of that practice and built its images into New Testament metaphors. Even today, Roman Catholics and Protestants who interpret the Bible literally cite John the Baptist referring to Jesus as "the Lamb of God, who takes away the sin of the world!" (John 1:29) In their own language they speak of our need to be "washed in the blood of the Lamb." They make the point that Jesus was God's perfect, supreme sacrifice because 1) he is God's Son who left his home in heaven to complete his Father's plan to save the world; 2) he was born of a virgin without male sperm and, thus, was untainted by sin through sex; 3) he never had a "dirty" thought or did a bad thing (as far as we know); and 4) he willingly submitted himself to humiliation and torture by a Roman death squad—all for your benefit and mine. What more could he have done for us? What more could we have asked of him?

With the sacrificial death of his son, the Church tells us, God satisfies not only his sense of justice (the sins of his children are paid for), but also his love (he wants his children to spend eternity with him in Heaven, and this makes it possible). In terms of God's reputation, his actions represent a trade-off: He sends his Son to be executed and looks callous, like the ancient Hebrew God, who demanded the murder of the children of tribes that got in His way. But in the same transaction, we can see him as loving, for he provides the only way people can be saved from his judgment. In other words, in this plan, God manages to have it both ways. We'll come back to this Christian motif of sacrifice in Chapter 12.

Catholicism and Mainline Protestantism

Roman Catholicism has its centuries-old prescriptions for surviving the predicament. Most of us know that Jesus' death dominates Catholic thought, and that traditional Catholics wear crucifixes. The faithful participate in an elaborate system of priest-led sacraments, or rites, at the center of which is the mass, or the ongoing daily reenactment of Jesus' death, in which the bread turns into Jesus' body and the wine into his blood. The Church sees *spiritual sacrifices* as a major pattern for living within the predicament. It reasons that, if God sacrificed his Son, and his Son sacrificed his life for us sinners, true Catholics will live lives of sacrifice. The more traditional Roman Church holds that those who attend its rites, believe its dogmas, do good works, and sacrifice for the good of the Church and God's world—including having lots of children—will be spiritually blessed in their daily lives by God and may qualify for God's eternal blessing and not go to Hell.

In the twenty-first century, Catholicism faces critical internal problems. Most traditional Catholics grew up before the radical reforms begun by Pope John XXIII and the Second Vatican Council (Vatican II 1962-1965). That the mass would not be done in Latin anymore but in the language of the people; that the laity would be more visible in the governance of local parishes; that the official hierarchy would show a bit of humility in relation to Protestantism—reforms like these shocked traditionalists. They have argued that these modernizing reforms caused widespread indifference to longtime Catholic customs, beliefs, and pious practices. They've also pointed to tenets of the council that contradict earlier papal statements regarding faith, morals, and doctrine. They once boasted about their "One True and Eternal Church." They now feel betrayed and lost.

With Vatican II, secularized, mainly younger Catholics jumped for joy; they celebrated the opening of the door to what they felt was fresh air in the Church. Today, many of those who once embraced Vatican II reforms and breathed that fresh air—and their descendants—want more. They continue to have trouble digesting some of the Church's timeworn rituals, its all-male power structure, its often fanciful dogma, and especially its clergy sex-abuse scandals compounded by shameful cover-ups. Everyone knows that liberated American Catholics do things the pope says not to do (practice artificial birth control, for one). Progressive American nuns have organized and pressed the Vatican for open dialogue about the role of women in the church, and the Vatican has attempted to muzzle them.

The Roman Church in this country, particularly since Vatican II, has generally supported science, aside from such issues as abortion and birth control. It's also helped lead the causes for equal rights for minorities, for economic and racial justice, for kindness toward the poor, and for peace, seen this day in the beautiful spirit of Pope Francis. As a result, an untold number of sentimental, traditional Catholics have left the church. At the very opposite, progressive end of the faith spectrum, many former church members call themselves "Recovering Catholics," saying they will struggle "one day at a time" to refrain from ever going back to what they rejected as demeaning, irrelevant religion. The Church suffers blows from its right and left.

Mainline Protestant denominations—American Baptist, Disciples of Christ, Episcopal, Lutheran, Methodist, Presbyterian, and United Church of Christ—have their own problems. Their members mainly are educated and try to make sense of inherited beliefs in this scientific, postmodern day. Many churches within each denomination are deeply divided in their understanding of scripture, the nature of God, sexuality—especially homosexuality—militarism, and interfaith cooperation. Some congregations are trying hard to help disheartened members and disillusioned former members find their way and pull their lives together; but the task is not easy.

These middle-of-the-road denominations have come to terms with science's view of origins. At the same time, their clergy continue to use a lot of the God-talk language that shows they remain sentimentally attached to the "enchanted forest." Their members typically move in and out of two different worlds, the supernatural on Sundays and the scientific the rest of the week.

These believers tend to revere the Bible as a source of inspiration and guidance. To varying degrees they believe Jesus and the writers were on to something of critical importance. They value the warmth of the love at the heart of Jesus' message. But they don't see miracles happening in their world and in their own lives like those they find in the Bible, and they don't worship their scriptures as the eternal Word of God. Fundamentalists think of them as *modernists*, liberal betrayers of the Bible, God and Christ.

Mainline denominations also shy away from the idea of a sacrificial atonement achieved by Jesus on the cross. They believe Jesus' self-giving is a demonstration of the role *agapaic* love plays in our ability to experience spiritual wholeness in the midst of the predicament. Most have some underlying assumption about heaven and perhaps hell, as well. But they break ties with fundamentalists and evangelicals not only over the Bible and what Jesus' death means but also over their strange, cataclysmic, end-of-the-world views, which we'll get to shortly.

Each mainline denomination exhibits its own style, and their congregations vary a bit in forms of worship, theology and social concern. Most churches carry on prescribed, traditional worship, with some of them holding alternate celebrations using other than stained-glass language and music not supported by the organ. Their members look for spiritual nourishment through both forms of worship, as well as small groups for Bible study and prayer, pastoral care during personal crises, working together on matters they deem important, and special seasonal celebrations, especially those of Advent, Epiphany, and Lent.

Most of these denominations also have caught the ecumenical spirit: the importance of cooperating with other churches in local projects and with councils of churches. A few engage in interfaith activities.

In times past, many in these churches worked in support of the Civil Rights, antiwar, and Women's Liberation movements. Today, most of them try in some way to help the poor and most vulnerable in our society. A small minority of denominations actually try to combat the root causes of inequity, the disregard of the environment, and violence in America. And a few confront our government's friendship with war, its bias in favor of the extremely wealthy, and its failure to address such threats as climate change. A small percentage of members in these churches find that working on such concerns provides the warmth or deep sense of purpose and spiritual fulfillment they need.

In centuries past, these mainline denominations founded most of the country's leading institutions of higher education. Their members played positive leadership roles in American life, including politics, business, science, the arts, and education. In 1965, when the U.S. population was 180 million, these churches together reached a membership peak of 31 million. In 2012, with the U.S. population at about 315 million, Church officials reported a sizable drop in combined membership to about 25 million.

For more specific information on any of these denominations, Google them.

Fundamentalism and the Peculiar Evangelicalism

I noted earlier that 150 million Americans take the ancient scriptures literally. Most of them identify themselves with fundamentalism and evangelicalism, the two largest, informal groups within Protestantism. Most in the latter group don't like being lumped in with the former, though they all call themselves "Bible-believing Christians."

Fundamentalism practices divisiveness. It insists that believers separate from nonbelievers. Believers invariably count on supernatural intervention through their prayers and hold to narrowly defined dogma based on literal interpretations of the Bible. They believe that nonbelievers, believers in other religions, and any others who disagree with them are blind to God's truth and unacceptable to God. When others challenge their beliefs, they try to ignore, or censor, intimidate, punish, and, in extreme cases, demonize and kill them. Most are not as fanatical as the Ku Klux Klan or Muslims bent on militant jihads, but many of them believe their God calls for violence in defense of and adherence to "God's truth." They have demonstrated this belief in their nearly universal approval of wars that mainly involve killing non-Christians, and in their extreme attacks on abortion clinics.

During most of the twentieth century, fundamentalists lived their narrow life in the shadow of mainstream American society. But in the 1990s, they left the sanctuaries of the Bible Belt (no longer a geographic area) and shrewdly took control of the Republican Party at almost every level. Fighting against embryonic stem cell research, abortion, the teaching of evolution, and equal rights for homosexuals, they are happy to be known as *anti-science*. They also are hell-bent, by their own admission, on changing America from a secular democracy to a theocracy: "the Christian nation God and our forebears meant it to be."

Their prominence in politics suffered serious blows in national elections, beginning in 2006. For years after that, through the Tea Party, they've held control of the House of Representatives. Financial and sexual scandals have tarnished their reputation, but their strange view of human nature continues to exert major influence on the American belief system and our understanding of spirituality.

Some evangelicals remain in mainline denominations, but most of them migrate toward independent churches and conservative denominations, the largest of which is Southern Baptist. As of 2012, it became the largest Protestant body in the United States, with a nearly 16 million membership, and is no longer confined to the South.

This brand of Protestantism deserves a closer look here, because of its strong influence on our American view of spirituality, on our national worldview, on our politics, especially through the Tea Party, and on so many millions of individual lives. Interestingly, while evangelicals and fundamentalists are strongly oriented to the ancient Bible, they see America as God's new *Holy Land*, "a city on a hill" (a phrase from Jesus in Matthew 5:14), and their religiosity often comes off as a sentimental patriotism. They seem to have no trouble letting the whole world hear them sing "God Bless America."

Evangelicals, as well as fundamentalists, accept the creation/fall-from-grace stories of Genesis, but they have their own interpretations of what we must do to survive the human predicament. Along with Catholics, they emphasize the death of Jesus' on the cross as a sacrifice on our behalf. Their view of how we tap into it for our eternal salvation, however, is dramatically different from that of Catholicism. Here's the idea: As the one who carries out God's plan, Jesus saves from eternal damnation all those who make the choice to place their trust in him to be their personal Savior. The need to believe that Jesus paid for both your original sin through Adam, and your personal sins, so you can go to heaven, is central to their worldview. To the troublesome question, "What if you've never heard of Jesus, or you have but don't choose to trust him?" they have a simple answer: "Pity. Go to hell."

As I noted earlier, the story of Jesus in the Gospels and the New Testament doesn't end with the cross. A couple of days after he is buried, God raises him from the dead (another act that makes God look good). Soon thereafter, Jesus has several weird encounters with his disciples, offers them some carry-it-on instructions, and bids them goodbye. He ascends up through the clouds into heaven, somewhere in outer space. There he sits down on a big throne at the right hand of God the Father. (I trust, once again, that you've heard enough about this scheme to know that I'm not pulling your leg.)

If this account strikes you as odd, look at the bizarre twist fundamentalists and evangelicals give to the end of the world, a vision not shared by Catholicism and mainline Protestant churches. These believers are led by Bible interpreters who discern that scripture divides the past, present and future into distinct historical periods, or *dispensations,* during which God relates to his people, the Jews and then Christians, differently. These periods began about 6000 years ago with Adam and Eve in Eden and run to a last-days dispensation that includes Jesus' return to earth (the Second Coming). *Dispensationalists* strive to get in correct order the several events at the end-time, and to their dismay, they disagree and divide over them.

They all say that at God's appointed time, one day soon, Jesus will come back to Earth for a second time and drop the curtain on history. He will draw true Christians up into the clouds with him (the *Rapture*). This spectacular rescue of fundamentalists and evangelicals will get them beyond the human predicament and take them directly to heaven's door. The Rapture also includes all the believers who have died before the Second Coming. They will be resurrected, as Jesus was, coming out of their graves and flying up to meet him in the sky, along with those alive at the time. God gives all these folk *spiritual bodies,* which fit them for heaven. I'm not sure what happens to believers who were cremated, but I'm sure they believe that God can put all the pieces together into whatever is a *spiritual body.* These believers base such ideas on a few strange passages in their Old Testament prophetic books, on some statements attributed to St. Paul, whom, scholars say, obviously expected Jesus' return during his lifetime, and on some weird symbolism in the last book in the Bible, the Revelation to John.

But that's not the end. Most *dispensationalists* believe that right after the Rapture will come a seven-year stretch during which all hell breaks loose on Earth (the Great Tribulation). Needless to say, this portends a terrible time for those "left behind." The book of Revelation offers murky symbolism at best, and *dispensationalist* Bible teachers differ about the order of these final events. In particular, they find little agreement as to when the Great Tribulation occurs. They all are certain, however, that it all ties in to the Last Judgment, when we all will receive rewards and punishments for how we've lived. (Objective scholars tell us that this idea originated with the ancient Zoroastrians.) Some of these teachers insist that Jesus and his followers will enjoy a peaceful thousand-year reign on Earth (the Millennium). Others are sure the Millennium occurs *before* the tribulation. Still others insist there won't be a Millennium at all. And they all believe they are right.

This rather freakish end-time scenario made its way into the popular American consciousness through the late 1990s smash literary success known as the *Left Behind* series. These novels, filled with catastrophic violence and romance (yes, flirting and some titillating hints of spicy sex) were written to warn you not to be "left behind" when Jesus returns for his own. According to Wikipedia, total sales for the series in 2013 have surpassed 65 million copies. Seven titles in the adult series have reached #1 on the bestseller lists for the *New York Times*, *USA Today*, and *Publishers Weekly*. The latest polls suggest that at least 40 million adult Americans believe that the biblical "signs of the times" show that in the next 50 years (maybe before you finish reading this book), Jesus will come down through the clouds from heaven as an end-time superhero, save his people, and defeat Satan. Because the scriptural symbols are, indeed, murky, to say the least, and predictors in the past have embarrassed themselves by setting dates, many evangelicals leave the timing *up in the air*, so to speak.

Several aspects of this worldview are troubling. For one, it makes some *dispensationalists* think that nuclear war would not be a bad idea. Mushroom clouds, they believe, could help trigger Jesus' victorious return to earth, which they await and want to help hasten. In sum, they think the purpose of being Christian is to prepare for Jesus' imminent *return* and escape the predicament to everlasting bliss (Google "Dispensationalism" to learn more).

Fundamentalists may fight among themselves about the order of these end-time events, but they are of one mind with evangelicals that Jesus is the only way to the heavenly afterlife. They are fond of quoting words attributed to Jesus himself: "I am the way, the truth and the life; no one comes to the Father but by me" (John 14:6). When Charlie Rose interviewed popular pastor and author Rick Warren on his PBS show, he asked Warren how evangelicals justified saying their loving God won't accept those who've never heard of Jesus but will send them all to hell to be forever tortured. Warren replied, "Don't ask me—ask Jesus. He's the one who said it," and quoted John 14:6. Later on we'll look at an entirely different way to interpret this verse.

Most of these believers dispassionately and without embarrassment assign to eternal fire not only followers of other religions but also secular humanists, pagans, atheists, heathen savages, Roman Catholics, liberal

Protestants and, as already noted, everyone who has never heard of Jesus. In the end, only those who trust in Jesus the way fundamentalists and evangelicals spell it out will get to be forever with God in heaven. And, literally, again, "To hell with everyone else."

Both Christian and Islamic fundamentalists give the distinct impression they think God cares about how they live. At the same time, they believe He primarily is interested in the eternal destiny of their souls. Even today they see Earth as a way station to heaven and believe that true religion exists to help people reach that destination. The life we have now is *a trust, a test and a temporary assignment.* Many morally sensitive believers and nonbelievers say the obsession of fundamentalist and evangelical leaders with the afterlife distracts their followers from dealing with the catastrophic crises we humans have created and is reason enough to reject such Christianity.

Several marks identify traditional Christianity in its fundamentalist and evangelical forms. Their adherents:

- Interpret the Bible literally as God's eternal, inerrant truth
- Affirm that their God is the one and only true God
- Proclaim the saving death and resurrection of Jesus
- Insist that their teachings are true and push them on others
- Require everyone to be "born again" as they see it
- Stress worshiping, praying and studying the Bible
- Assign true believers to Heaven and everyone else to Hell

If you tell devotees of traditional Christianity that you have trouble making sense of their worldview, or you'd like some evidence their claims are true, they will tell you God revealed His plan in the Bible a long time ago. When you ask them how they know the Bible is God's Word, they will tell you it says it is. They also will tell you the Bible has read their hearts and, they believe, changed their lives for the better.

I don't think advocates of the narrow expressions of Christianity are stupid, though I do think they believe some stupid things. What concerns me is their failure to question their inherited teachings, open their minds to new knowledge, and think "outside the biblical box." Sadly, in many places, if clergy or lay persons have done some thinking, they are reticent to challenge Church authorities for fear of being put down and shunned, or even excommunicated. To feel secure with their *ultimate truth*, they cannot allow room for a single doubt. And they feel that to question the Bible or their leaders would be to slap God in the face and incur His wrath.

A longtime recovered-fundamentalist friend is fond of saying, "I still see the *fun* in *fun*damentalism; I see the *dam(n)* in fun*dam*entalism; but I'll be damned if I see the *mental* in funda*mental*ism."

In the end, of course, the *intellectual dysfunction* of fundamentalism is no joke and ought not to be ignored. Its advocates reject new knowledge, unbiased thinking, and rational dialogue. And they are up to a lot of mischief. In 2013, Texas school boards, controlled by Christian fundamentalists, asked teachers not to teach critical thinking, because it causes students to criticize their parents and churches. Based on scriptural teachings, traditional believers continue to demean certain groups and rob them of their rights. When asked why women aren't worthy of equal status with men and why homosexuals deserve to be put to death, they quote a verse of scripture and beat a hasty retreat behind the closed door they label *faith*. When they do this, I suggest, they dehumanize real human beings, undermine respect for truth, insult their religion's best insights, and, indeed, betray the spirit of Jesus.

If you are looking for spiritual depth and personal fulfillment, but you also are a thinking person who is repulsed by sentimentality and closed-mindedness, your options are limited. Some dogmas in American Christianity may strike you as weird. But thousands of cults that arose in the past couple of centuries in America in response to the looming death of God and the breakdown of biblical faith hold beliefs that make traditional Christianity look downright rational. Some of these sects are small and nearly invisible. Others have been better known in certain regions of the country. Still others have attracted a lot of attention and have followers in the millions. You have heard of them, though you probably can't tell me much about them.

Four *Born-in-America*, nineteenth-century sects stand out:

1) **The Church of Christ, Scientist**. This church's main deviation from Christian teachings is its claim that sin, pain and death are unreal. We know it as Christian Science. Christians say it is not Christian; and scientists contend it is not science.

2. **The Church of Jesus Christ of Latter-Day Saints.** Joseph Smith saw God and had a visit by an angel, who helped him write the Book of Mormon and found this church. We know it best for its Salt Lake City tabernacle, its huge choir, and Mitt Romney. Few non Mormons are aware of its strange teachings.

3) **Seventh-day Day Adventists.** This church worships on Saturday, rather than Sunday. The believed the world would end in 1844. They hold some other bizarre beliefs. To their credit, Adventists have a solid humanitarian record and an impressive health care system, the largest in the country.

4) **Jehovah's Witnesses.** This group holds a number of things contrary to Christianity, which gives it its cult status. Believers probably have been to your door, trying to convert you. Their end-time predictions say that only 144,000 Jehovah's Witnesses will be saved from God's final judgment.

All of these sects reports a substantial membership, fervently peddle their spiritual wares wherever they can, and seek your total attention, commitment, and loyalty. Not one of them shows serious respect for science, and each shares the self-important mindset of fundamentalism: *We have the latest revealed truth from God, and those who differ with us are dead wrong.* Google them for more information.

When you ask any fundamentalist or *cultic* type why you should accept their self-serving, preposterous claims, they will admit they don't have proof for them—"You must take them *by faith*." We'll come back to this, but first look briefly at a couple of softer versions of narrow Christianity.

Pentecostalism

American Pentecostalism, an emotional first cousin to fundamentalism, originated in 1906, in Los Angeles, as a missionary movement, with a handful of believers. In the earlier twentieth century, outsiders called them *holy rollers* for tumbling in church aisles, purportedly under the influence of the Holy Spirit. A century later Pentecostalism claims 20 million members in the United States, including one million in New York City alone. Observers estimate that half of their number today are former Roman Catholic Hispanics.

As does fundamentalism, Pentecostalism sees the Bible as the Word of God. Its main goal is to get people saved from hell and into heaven. To deal with life today, however, its leaders don't call so much for belief in elaborate doctrines as for personal encounters with the supernatural Holy Spirit. They stress the new things the Spirit is doing and contend that what's in the heart counts more than what's in the head.

Pentecostal worship encourages spontaneity and ecstatic experiences that include supernatural healing and speaking in unintelligible tongues. They see such phenomena as signs of true baptism by the Spirit. Their members have little interest in science, secular progress, and critical thinking, which separates them from those in mainline Protestant churches. They see themselves as Evangelicals but with a more charismatic, or Spirit-centered style. Some Pentecostal denominations and their splinter groups hold membership in the National Association of Evangelicals, but they like to think of themselves as less theological and more spiritual than the other churches.

For most educated Americans, Pentecostals are hidden in the open. The closest most older folk have come to Pentecostalism was watching Oral Roberts and Jimmy Swaggart on TV in the 1960s-80s. Pentecostalism has suffered its share of sexual scandals; but its sensational, continuing growth worldwide—it now constitutes 25 percent of all the world's Christians--makes some dub the twenty-first century as *The Age of the Holy Spirit*. We must note that in many America's cities, it is the

Pentecostals who leave the comforts of their homes for the hard streets to minister compassionately to prostitutes, addicts, the poor, and others who are hurting and trapped. Visit Penecostal churches to experience a lot of emotional warmth, but know that you'll be asked to check your brains at the door.

The Megachurches

American evangelicalism and Pentecostalism mostly grow their own churches. They also, however, have informally joined to help spawn the glitzy megachurch movement, a loose network of nearly 2,000 mostly nondenominational, super-sized churches. About 50 churches on the list have Sunday attendance ranging from 10,000 to 47,000. Some 3,000 Roman Catholic parishes have 2,000 or more attendants at Mass on Sunday, but they are not part of the megachurch movement.

The largest megachurch in the United States is Lakewood Church in Houston, Texas, with more than 40,000 formal members. The largest megachurch in the world is South Korea's Yoido Full Gospel (Pentecostal) Church, with more than one million members as of 2012. In reality, this megachurch functions more like its own denomination, having spawned a couple of dozen gigantic congregations.

Most American megachurches thrive in Sunbelt city suburbs as "seeker churches." They look to attract unhappy mainline Protestants and Catholics, as well as the unhappy nonreligious who are seeking structure, instruction in religious and spiritual matters, a sense of belonging, and a spiritual community that appears to be successful. They have aimed particularly at younger people and couples, who might think that churches offering programs for their teens and kids will help solidify their families. They usually are user-friendly and full-service, often featuring such amenities as Starbucks cafes, ATMs, game rooms for children, bowling alleys, gyms, ball teams, and cleaners. To help members with a sense of belonging in such large congregations, they stress small groups for activities such as yoga, exercise, sports teams, meditation, and, yes, even prayer and Bible study.

In line with the American business model of *bigger is better*, megachurches look on numerical growth and sheer size as signs both of God's approval and blessing and of secular success. Their pastors tend to be savvy about marketing, and many have television ministries. Their worldview often features some form of the "prosperity gospel," the appealing ideas that God wants you to be rich and happy (poverty is a curse), and, if you will believe that God will prosper you, He will. Unlike pastors in most conservative churches, megachurch preachers tend to speak everyday language rather than "churchese." They focus on members' marriages, parenting, health concerns, and finances. They want to help members be good people, feel good and get to "the good life," both here and in the hereafter.

Perhaps it's the Pentecostal influence, or simply a concern not to project a stuffy image, but hard theological *thinking* is conspicuously absent in megachurches. Rituals, kept simple, are done with shouts and smiles—church is to be mainly fun. One critic says that because megachurches put theological cookies on the lower shelf and don't expect members to think critically or ask difficult worldview questions, their belief system is "about a mile wide and an inch deep."

Unlike Evangelical churches, megachurches usually do not display the cross, or talk about sacrifice. They also, unlike progressive Catholic and Protestant churches, avoid confronting controversial social issues. Critics contend that they compromise Christianity by tailoring their ministries to the marketplace and to pop culture. Some megachurches do push the *prosperity gospel.* In doing so, critics say, they encourage members to focus inwardly and get all wrapped up in their own wants. To be fair, some megachurches, while not addressing the root causes of poverty, violence or despair, have set up divorce counseling services, *handout* ministries to the poor, and drug rehab programs for youth. Like service organizations, local adult education programs, fitness centers, and secular therapeutic groups, they undoubtedly help a number of people hold their lives together.

Most of these churches show little concern for doctrinal conformity. Beneath their hip facades, however, lies the Bible-believing mindset that interprets literally the dramatic stories of scripture, and holds to the Last Days scenario of evangelicalism, including Jesus' descent from heaven, and to the idea of an eternal heaven and hell. If you are well informed, thinking and care about making serious sense out of what is real, most megachurches could make you throw up, faint, or run out screaming.

The megachurch movement has not formed a new denomination or sect of any sort, but it is a significant part of American Protestant Christianity. Though relatively few in number, its churches have been growing by leaps and bounds and in 2014 hold close to 10 percent of Protestant worshipers on Sunday mornings. Some observers believe that they foreshadow America's religion of the future and, in one sense, they are a new *species* of church.

Whenever someone attempts to broadly characterize organizations, movements, or belief systems, particularly those with which he or she may not be impressed, there is a danger of distortion. I trust I've not fallen victim to that danger with those I've reviewed here. I am disappointed with the evangelicalism that held a place in my past, but I'm also aware that it is a movement more nuanced than I've had space to describe. Even as many of its leaders defend the narrowness I've described, some show signs of moderation and heartfelt concern for those who are being ignored and gored by social powers.

To complete our exploring of worldviews that claim answers to life's challenges and promise spiritual enrichment, listen with me to some venerable voices from far away, now increasingly in competition with today's American Christianity. While these voices do not impact our culture as strongly as the dominant Christian worldview, you undoubtedly are aware of them, and they deserve at least brief attention.

Can there be any doubt that, during the last 25 centuries, Buddha, Christ or Mohammed have been the most honored, idolized, adored, discussed ... figures in history?

G. Krishna

The most important characteristic of the Eastern worldview—one could almost say the essence of it—is the awareness of the unity and mutual interrelation of all things and events, the experience of all phenomena in the world as manifestations of a basic oneness

Fritjof Capra

The more we can do to support and promulgate the intellectual traditions of the Abrahamic faiths—of Judaism, Christianity and Islam—the better armed we will be to fight fundamentalism.

Jon Meacham

CHAPTER 7:

OTHER OLD WORLDVIEWS

We have been reviewing Christianity's major claims to truth and solutions to our spiritual needs. So far, we've covered pre-Vatican II Roman Catholicism, Protestantism's centrist expressions, and fundamentalism and Evangelicalism. Their worldviews have combined to dominate religion in America and, from our nation's beginnings, they have butted heads with one another. Now, for the first time, as we move further into Millennium III, Christianity must compete with other ancient belief systems that are expanding their visibility in the U.S., with both mouths and arms wide open.

Look at three non-Christian, theological or philosophical worldviews that have enlarged the landscape of American religion.

Judaism

We rightly look at the religion that forms the foundation of Christianity and Islam. Judaism and Jewish history stand on a remarkable religious and spiritual foundation some 4000 years old. As noted earlier, about 2000 years ago, the Jews dropped animal sacrifices as the way to please God and began emphasizing education, religious tradition, and obedience to God's laws. As do some Christians, most religious Jews believe that the Ten Commandments delivered by Moses apply to all peoples at all times in all places; they are not up for discussion and deserve to be enforced by civil as well as religious authorities.

Judaism in America today, takes three basic forms:

1) **Orthodox.** This branch stands as the thesis, or starting point, for Judaism. It is spiritually rooted in Jewish

history, mysticism, and piety, and maintains strict obser-
vance of Jewish law from the Hebrew Bible, religious
pursuits in the temple, and old-time distinctive dress.
Strongly controlled by men, it gives women second-class
status and has no women rabbis. Politically, it leans to
the right, or conservative side, especially with regard to
the state of Israel.

2) **Reform.** This branch stands as the antithesis to Orthodoxy for religious Jews. It holds to the secular core values of pluralism, modernity, equality, science, and social
justice, and attempts to merge certain Jewish traditions
with contemporary lifestyles. Women mostly enjoy equal
status with men in the temple, and the branch has been
happy to ordain women rabbis. Politically, it leans to the
left, though many turn to the right when it comes to
Israel.

3) **Conservative.** This somewhat modern branch seeks
to synthesize in a middle course what it considers the
extremes of Orthodox Judaism on the right and Reform
Judaism on the left. It keeps many traditional elements of
Judaism, while allowing for some reasonable moderniza-
tion and rabbinical development, including the ordina-
tion of women rabbis. It tends to lean to the right politically, particularly with regard to Israel.

The more orthodox the form of Judaism, the more mystical its
spirituality. The Hasidim, a branch of Orthodox Judaism, promote
spirituality through the internalization of Jewish mysticism as the
fundamental aspect of the faith. They stress personal piety over learning
and legalism. Hasidic teachings cherish the sincerity and concealed
holiness of the common folk, and hold them as equals of the scholarly
elite. Orthodoxy also offers the Kabbalah, a body of mystical teachings
of rabbinical origin most often based on an arcane interpretation of the
Hebrew Scriptures. The teachings have gained popular attention today
through their adoption by some showbiz celebrities (Madonna, for one).

Other adherents include some people who are not Jewish—creating, perhaps, the spirituality chic I referred to earlier, which annoys serious Jewish mystics.

Many Jews today find roots in the rich writings of their ancient, often heroic prophets, who were secular mavericks. They held a strong bias against religion while railing against national injustice and neglect of the poor. With strong spiritual values, they spoke up for underdogs who were always getting the short end of the political and economic stick. It's they who told the rich and powerful that the poor are worthy of protection. It is they who held forth the principles that cause us to insist today that all humans are worthy of food, shelter, decent medical care, education, and trial by a jury of their peers.

Today, of course, not everyone in our culture once dominated by the Hebrew worldview pays attention to the prophets, especially the rich and powerful. But Reform Jews, in particular, fall readily into activism for education and justice—at their best they identify what is broken in the world and try to fix it. They are among the strongest participants in the cutting-edge struggles for human rights, health care, the environment, and peace. And it shouldn't surprise us they hold prominent roles in such a growing national movement as the Network of Spiritual Progressives, begun in 2005 (Google it).

Many American Jews hold only a nominal relationship with Judaism, or have dropped out of religious life altogether. They tend to find their identity and spiritual enrichment not in Judaism itself, but in loyalty to the state of Israel and in Jewish culture, especially its special rituals and festive holidays.

From among an estimated seven million American Jews, a disproportionately high percentage have distinguished themselves by excellence in academia, the arts, business, politics, finance, medicine and other sciences. Their success, plus the fact that some traditional, religious Jews still see themselves as "God's chosen people," thinking they were *chosen because they were choice,* that is, better than others, rather than *chosen to serve.* This irritates many non-Jews, including traditional Christians, who have held their faith to be superior to Judaism. Shamefully, at times, irritation has blossomed into hatred of Jews. Making matters worse, Christian fundamentalists have perpetuated the notion that it was the Jews who killed Jesus, thereby fanning the flames of full-blown antisemitism. In some parts of the country this moral sickness, right along with racism, has abated. In other parts it still thrives.

In the mid-twentieth century, Christian fundamentalists began concerted efforts to convert Jews through such movements as Jews for Jesus (Google it). At the same time, in some areas, mainline Protestant churches and synagogues went so far as to begin engaging in interfaith dialogues and sharing community service projects.

From its beginnings in this country, Judaism has lost members because of their assimilation by marriage into Christianity or secular culture. At the same time, Judaism in one form or another has absorbed some former Christians and secularists—through marriage, the influence of friends, or the search for spiritual fulfillment. Recently, perhaps for the first time, the Church seems to have realized that, thanks especially to interfaith marriages, young people reared in the church not only are dropping out of it but, in some cases, especially in urban areas, also are converting to Judaism. We can't point to serious efforts by Jews to convert Christians, but in an America that is more tolerant than ever before, churches are aware of losing members here and there to the Jewish faith.

Eastern Philosophy

Buddhism, Confucianism, Hinduism, Jainism, Shintoism, and Taoism all originated in the Far East but are in our midst today. It isn't easy to summarize their worldviews, because these traditions have conflicting beliefs and a myriad of sectarian divisions. They do hold in common, however, a concern for knowing the mind—what it is, how it works, what its powers are. They believe we are what we think, and they invariably see us as "prisoners of our minds." Some are at the forefront of attempts today to understand how meditation changes our brains.

We tend to view Eastern seekers as religious devotees, because many who claim to be followers treat their beliefs as a religion; they give them special status as if they are the ultimate or only truths. Thoughtful spokespersons for these beliefs, however, say they serve simply as guideposts for a way of life—which links them more closely to what we normally mean by *philosophy*.

Of these philosophies, Hinduism has the largest following worldwide, an estimated 900 million. We Americans are most aware of Buddhism, an offshoot of Hinduism, with 360 million adherents, and which originated according to the following tradition:

> The rich Hindu prince, Siddhartha Gautama, was born about 500 years before Jesus. As a young man, exposed to and stricken by the world's misery, he left wealth behind and set out to find a way to inner peace, or Nirvana, through enlightenment. He held that we create our own evil and suffering by trying to satisfy earthly desires, rather than detaching ourselves from them.
>
> As a way to escape desires, suffering, unhappiness, and bad *karma* (the emotional, moral and psychological baggage that builds up in us over successive lives) he taught the Eight-fold Path: 1) right thinking, 2) right aim, 3) right speech, 4) right action, 5) right living, 6) right effort, 7) right mindfulness, and 8) right concentration.

By repeating the word *right*, I take him to emphasize behavior appropriate to human nature. With this teaching, Siddhartha became Gautama Buddha (The Enlightened One) and established wisdom and compassion as the twin pillars of Buddhism. Some Americans, fed up with Western religion but without having joined any Buddhist organizations, have sought to build their lives on these two pillars, and, when pressed, may say they are Buddhists.

Unlike adherents to the Western religions, those who seriously embrace Eastern philosophies don't care about where the universe or we humans came from. They also don't buy the mythologies and dogmas of the Judeo-Christian tradition, with which we are so familiar. In contrast to the view that humans spend a lifetime on earth and then go off to some mysterious other place, followers of the Eastern traditions see our existence as a perpetual cycle of birth, suffering, death, and rebirth (reincarnation), which leads ultimately to a total riddance of desire and release from the cycle of rebirth.

The strong emphasis in Eastern philosophy on compassion and nonviolence, which are basic marks of *agape*, are not necessarily practiced fully in Eastern societies. But as core teachings they sit in sharp contrast to the traditional Western religions that tend to condone and even help perpetuate certain forms of social and political violence, such as preemptive war, capital punishment and terrorism.

Some Buddhists retain metaphysical dimensions of their religion built up over two and a half millennium. If we press other Buddhists, particularly younger ones in this country, to identify their religious view, they reluctantly tell us they are pagans, animists, pantheists, atheists or agnostics (if need be, go back to the list in Chapter 3, or do some Googling). They claim to be secular, or spiritual in a *nonsupernatural* way. Western religions stress religious rituals and practices; Eastern worldviews hold that human beings attain spiritual self-realization by testing their beliefs in everyday experience. Buddhists also don't stress teachings about God but, instead, produce monks and nuns, or spiritually dedicated, disciplined persons who, through meditation, pursue wholeness by integrating what they see as mind, body, and spirit.

Westerners have criticized Eastern philosophers for teaching people to ignore human suffering, rather than addressing its causes and working to relieve it. But Vietnamese Zen Buddhist Thich Nhat Hanh and the Tibetan Buddhist Dalai Lama, both internationally respected teachers and secular Buddhists, have long led their followers to confront the hardest of human rights and social justice abuses. Back in the 1960s, trying to shut down the oppressive South Vietnamese government, Buddhist monks engaged in public self-immolation. In 2007, Buddhist monks risked their own lives to lead mass protest rallies aimed at revealing to the world the political tyranny of Myanmar's government. And, in just the four years from 2009 to 2013, no fewer than 120 monks and nuns have set themselves on fire to call attention to China's oppression of Tibetans. During the same period, too, untold numbers have been put in jail.

Until the last half of the twentieth century, mainstream America knew little of Asian ways, because of language barriers, geographical distances, and meager immigration opportunities. In the 1970s, thanks to changes in immigration law, great numbers of Asians began coming to live in the United States, giving them increased visibility. Quickly, the novelty and exotic nonreligious side of their spirituality charmed secular and nominally religious people, particularly on the West Coast. Despite that charm, the longtime absence in the Eastern worldview of a dedication to science, its association with many devotees who embrace ancient superstitions, and its reputed unwillingness to address social problems kept it from widespread adoption as a full-blown belief system. Only recently has the East concerned itself seriously with science.

Buddhism today claims an impressive three million serious practitioners in the United States. Without practicing the religious traditions of Buddhism, many non-Asian, non-Buddhist Americans practice the likes of Transcendental Meditation and yoga. They borrow these Buddhist techniques to augment their own Western practices to relieve the stress that comes with living a frenetic, rapidly-changing, postmodern life inside the predicament.

These borrowings from the East are not without an ironic twist, however. They are taking place at the same time that our media-exported materialism, which drives industry and free enterprise, and thus the foreign trade of goods, continues to increase its influence in the Far East. As Japan and Korea have done for decades, China now competes with our economy and materialistic way of life. So while the West, looking for spiritual solace and equilibrium, tries to calm down, slow down, and breathe deeply, the East picks up its pace to enter the rat race of competitive global markets.

Back in 1887, Rudyard Kipling began his poem, *The Ballad of East and West*, with, "Oh, East is East and West is West, and never the twain shall meet ..." Someone might have told Kipling, "Never say never in the future tense," for perhaps in ways he *never* could have imagined, his *twain*, indeed are meeting today.

The Other Islam

You may not be thinking of adopting Muslim spiritual practices, but it is important to have an informed picture of the followers of Islam.

As with Asians, since the 1970s, we've seen a massive influx of Muslims from the Far East and the Middle East. In 2014, we have about three million followers of Mohamed in the United States (almost 1 percent of our population). Since 9/11, our Muslim population has jumped dramatically. Mosques as well as Eastern temples have popped up in towns and cities all over the country, including in the Southeastern Bible Belt. So both Islam and Eastern philosophies bring us face-to-face with worldview options new to us and about which most of us know little.

Because of 9/11, and the fact that Muslim extremists have sought to terrorize us, a fear and loathing of Islam has smothered the minds of most Americans. I suggest you not let this popular *Islamophobia* control you. You need not tolerate Muslim fanatics, but you cannot view the Islamic world simply through the eyes of our media, which report little about Islam that is positive along with all that is negative about its extremists. You cannot be spiritually whole while judgmentally negative and out of touch with the truth.

Islam arose some 600 years after Jesus. Today's adherents total almost a fourth of world population. We've already noted that this third great theistic religion accepts the stories of Creation and the Fall that are found in the Bible's book of Genesis. To transcend the human predicament created by the disobedience of Adam and Eve, Muslims hold to the Quran—their own scriptures—and its strict moral codes concerning personal behavior and family life.

The Quran orders Muslims to follow faithfully a strict routine of prayer, five times a day, as well as to offer their individual prayers in private. It insists they give alms to the poor, which takes the form of an annual tax on wealth, and requires them to fast in daylight hours during the month of Ramadan. It also calls them to participate at least once in the annual five-day pilgrimage to the high plains of Arafat outside the sacred city of Mecca in Saudi Arabia, unless this obligation is waived due to a hardship. Many devout Muslims save money all their lives for this journey, and some make it more than once.

Muslims believe God rewards their faithfulness both by prospering them here and now and by giving them a blissful afterlife in paradise. Their faithfulness involves jihad, the idea of *striving to do God's will*— that is, to be virtuous, establish justice and ... defend Islam. Sadly, some fundamentalist Muslim rulers have used the idea of jihad to legitimize holy wars to expand their empires. Some Muslim fanatics have used it to justify suicide bombings and other forms of terrorism.

Americans today tend to see Islam as a violent religion and all Muslims as *jihadist* terrorists. It's true that a few verses in the Quran depict Allah telling the faithful to kill nonbelievers. But you also find this in the Bible. The book of Exodus tells us that Israel's God "makes sport" of the Egyptians by sending nasty plagues on them, including killing their firstborn, and then he drowns their army in the Red Sea. In the book of Joshua, which records what follows the successful exodus from Egypt, God tells Israel to storm the Promised Land and kill every member of the idolatrous tribes, including women and children (early *ethnic cleansing*, perhaps?). God also instructs Israel's leaders to see that homosexuals and unfaithful wives are stoned to death. The widely respected historian of religion Karen Armstrong, citing Church-sponsored wars over the centuries, all justified by the Bible, reminds us that Christians have a far worse record of terror than Muslims and that demonizing Islam itself is hypocritical and unjust.

Violent Islamic fanatics actually make up a tiny fraction of one percent of the world's Muslims. They clash with their own moderates as well as with modernity and with non-Muslims. This draws them ugly media attention and implants negative images of Islam itself in the consciousness of the world, particularly Israel, Europe, and the United States. Despite the fact that, unlike Judaism and Christianity, Islam has never gone through a reformation or something similar to the Enlightenment, the overwhelming majority of Muslims, including those in our country, are peaceloving and moderate in their faith. As they embrace Islamic rituals and its moral code, they affirm modernity, cooperate in interfaith endeavors, and want Islam to play a positive role in the secular world. Some moderates, at risk to their own lives, do speak out against the barbaric practices of Muslim extremists. It could remind you of what whites in the South have faced in confronting the "Christian" Ku Klux Klan.

I conclude this chapter by noting that I have thought it important to examine Judaism, Eastern philosophies, and Islam not only because they merit inclusion in any survey of influential worldviews, but also because these traditions seek to attract marginally Christian and nonreligious Americans who might find appealing a new, spiritually-based, way of life. If you are such an American, or your interest has been piqued, don't forget that by simply Googling in a key word you can put at your fingertips a wealth of information on any of these worldviews.

This leads us to another powerful take on reality that you'd ordinarily think would have nothing to do with your spiritual side. You may be in for a surprise.

The antidote to bad religion is good science.

Steven Landsburg

Science is the record of dead religions.

Oscar Wilde

Innocence about science is the worst crime today.

C.P. Snow

Most people when deciding whether to take a new job, embark on a divorce, or simply plan a holiday will not seek divine guidance, but rather discuss with themselves or others the issues of cause and effect.

Jim Herric

CHAPTER 8:

THE GLORIES OF SCIENCE

Method and Content

Scientists admit to ignorance. They know they don't know certain things about the natural realm, and they are curious. They look on science as the method by which you have the best possible chance to make sure that what you learn corresponds to what is real, or is true. It requires a skeptical state of mind. Their *inductive* method begins with asking questions. It then asks you to do research and construct a theory, or even a guess. It then involves testing your theory by doing trial-and-error experiments, analyzing data, drawing a conclusion, and then publishing your results to peers for them to examine, criticize and either reject, modify or confirm. Scientists consider this method crucial—it replaces for them the long-practiced, inadequate *deductive* method that for so long dominated Western thought and on which religion and philosophy still lean.

When I refer to science I'm assuming its loyalty to this method. But *science* also is the body of knowledge acquired by this method. Science constitutes a worldview that includes a coherent set of answers to our three big questions: "Where did everything come from? Why is life such a predicament? What will it take for me to live my best possible life?" It is the content of the worldview with which we're mainly concerned in this chapter.

Until early in the twentieth century, the biggest ideas in the scientific worldview came in the sixteenth century from Galileo Galilei; in the seventeenth century from Isaac Newton; in the nineteenth century from

Charles Darwin; and in the twentieth century from Albert Einstein. To identify their contributions in the simplest terms:

Galileo: Earth is not the center of the universe.
Newton: Gravity applies throughout the universe.
Darwin: Life forms evolve, from simple to complex, by natural selection.
Einstein: The theories of Special and General Relativity.

These scientific discoveries dramatically shifted the foundation on which the Western worldview would stand. For answers to the great questions of origins and nature, rather than look to a supernatural God, these scientists examined the natural, or secular, order. As a result, they've brought us a lot of *light*.

Why do away with God? Increasing numbers of scientists insist that their observations and tests yield no evidence of an intelligent Creator God, that their evidence actually flies in the face of the idea, and that to put God in the mix would mess with the reliability of any findings. Cosmologists say that all they find in space is an expanding yet purposeless material universe. It's this secular view of reality that makes most traditional believers fear the ongoing march of science, in the same way vampires dread the coming of the dawn.

Many observers think science already has put a dagger through the heart of what we know as religion. Because of modern science, we're the first age in history wherein nations construct culture without regard to whether God exists. Scientists say they understand why, in the distant past, people invented gods to explain the mysteries of nature. They also say we have no excuse today. It's true there are scientists who profess to believe in a god, or a mysterious, higher power, or force, of some sort. Some of them find comfort in staying connected to a religion. But their belief doesn't rise from their scientific endeavors, and, as I've already noted, gods don't fit easily into the materialistic, scientific worldview.

Scientists remind us, however, that just one short century ago we were groping in the darkness of ignorance and superstition about where the universe came from and what its nature is. As they point out, it is science that taught us that Earth is round, not flat; that our tiny planet revolves around the sun rather than the sun around it; and that we stand not at the center of the universe but near the edge of a rather ordinary galaxy among billions of others. Because of the evidence science has rechecked again and again, every high school graduate who has paid attention and looked without prejudice at these claims remains confident that science has "nailed it."

The Fascinating Universe

If I ask you, "where did everything come from?," and you relate to traditional religion, and your quick answer is, "From God the Creator," I ask you to think for a moment about what cosmologists have been telling us about our strange, beautiful and immense cosmos: "The universe isn't much larger than we always thought; it always will be much larger than we are able to imagine." Here are a few of their staggering figures; see if your brain will absorb them without breaking into pieces, bursting into flame, or blowing steam from your ears:

- Light travels in a vacuum, or in the emptiness of inter-stellar space, at 186,282.397 miles per second, or almost 700 million miles in an hour. That makes what we call a *light-year*—how far light travels in one earthly year—5.88 *trillion* miles. (Comedian Steven Wright asks, "Okay, so what's the speed of dark?")

- Keep in mind that a trillion is a thousand billion (a 1 followed by 12 zeroes). And scientists talk of an observable universe 14 billion—not thousand, not million, but *billion*—*light years* (not miles) across. Can your brain grasp this distance?

- Earth orbits one star in the Milky Way galaxy, which comprises some 200 billion stars. Our galaxy is 100,000 *light years* across (that's 100,000 times 5,880,000,000,000 miles in a year's travel). It's 20,000 light years thick, and its black hole is 27,000 light years away from us.

- Our Sun is 93 million miles from us, or about 8 1/3 light-minutes away. That's not very far in cosmic space. The next nearest star to us is but 4 1/4 light-*years* away (*not* light-minutes, hours or days, but *years*). But, again, not far as space goes. If you and I want to represent the distance between that nearby star and earth, we would have to stand 35,000 miles from each other, which is impossible, but ... use your imagination.

- The beautiful, spiral Sombrero Galaxy in the constellation Virgo is *28 million* light years from Earth, has *800 billion* suns and is 50,000 *light years* across. Can you imagine this?

- The findings of the Hubble Space Telescope point to the existence of at least *125 billion* galaxies in our universe. Galaxies can contain up to a *trillion* stars of varied sizes. Some of those stars are so large that one of the smaller galaxies could be placed inside them.

- Astronomers tell us that the most distant objects they see are about *11-12 billion light-years* (again, *not* miles) from us, and that the edges of the universe we look to are *13-15 billion light-years* away.

- I don't know who's counting, or how, but some scientists have estimated there are *25 times more stars* in the universe than grains of sand *on all the beaches of the world.*

These mind-boggling, awe-inspiring reports by scientists are not guesswork, science fiction, or a hoax. No one's making up these figures. Yes, question the details, but know that these astounding numbers are firmly in the ballpark. It's important to see this, for a healthy worldview must be based on the facts about our universe as well as our nature as humans.

The large majority of Americans, surveys tell us, still believes in "the Man Upstairs" their grandparents talked about. They base such belief on the ancient, Judeo/Christian worldview, with its one-among-many tribal God, whom it credits with having made the heavens and the Earth. So, here's the question: How does such a God operating in an ancient flat-earth, three-deck universe fit with the kind of universe pictured above? I'm not the first to suggest that our now well-established knowledge of the cosmos, of which people in ancient times could not have begun to dream, shakes the foundations of traditional monotheism. No, it does not disprove the existence of a transcendent Power, or Spirit, or other nonmaterial reality, but it certainly challenges the West to rethink its attachment to a celestial yet pedestrian Daddy figure.

Another Bizarre Environment

While postmodern cosmologists have been measuring the far reaches of the universe, other scientists, thinking really small, have come up with equally astonishing findings that challenge science as well as religion. Before Einstein's radical insights into the interaction of gravity, the speed of light and what he termed *space-time*, science held to the brilliant discovery of Newton that "the universe is governed solely by physical law." Then, influenced by Einstein and aided by vastly improved electronic microscopes, physicists in the 1920s introduced what they came to call *quantum theory,* or *quantum mechanics,* or *quantum physics.* The quantum field pertains to the subatomic world, where things are much too tiny to see with the naked eye.

Science has long held that all things are made of atoms, and that two or more atoms in a working arrangement form molecules, the physical building blocks of the material universe. The staggering distances in the cosmos are reported by scientists who've been looking, as it were, *up and out.* Bill Bryson, in his *A Short History of Nearly Everything*, gives us some *gee-whiz* information about atoms found by physicists who look, as it were, *down and in*:

- At sea level and 32 degrees Fahrenheit, a pocket of air the size of a sugar cube contains about *45 billion billion* molecules.
- One million carbon atoms could line up across *a human hair.*

- To see *the atoms in a drop of water* you'd have to enlarge the drop until it was the size of a lake *fifteen miles across.*
- If an apple is magnified to the size of the earth, then the atoms in the apple are approximately the size of the original apple.

Atoms are small, are they not? Do you think an atom is as tiny as anything can be? Surely you've heard that every atom has a nucleus. If you haven't, I hope you're sitting down when I tell you that, according to quantum physicists, the nucleus of an atom, although only one millionth of a billionth the size of the atom (the atom itself is mainly empty space), is fantastically dense. So, if you enlarged an atom to the size, say, of Yankee Stadium, the nucleus, high above second base, would be only as big—or as small—as a marble; but the marble would be thousands of times heavier than the stadium.

Now squeeze into your brain the fact that protons and neutrons, even dramatically smaller particles, exist inside the atom's minuscule nucleus. Inside them, we find the smaller gluons and quarks. Then think of the tiniest solar electron *neutrinos,* which scientists say mostly emanate from the sun and are constantly passing through the earth. They are so small, fast, and numerous that more than 50 trillion of them pass through the human body every second.

The subatomic world seems as tiny as the cosmos is huge. But quantum physicists find it much weirder. They've learned that atoms are active rather than passive, and that light isn't what they long had thought it was (it comes in particles as well as waves). As startling as anything, they discovered that electrons, the other particles we associate with the atom's nucleus, act like swirling clouds, actually not in, but around the nucleus; and their movements are seemingly *lawless.* At any given moment, quantum physicists can never be certain of the speed or the paths electrons will assume. But here's what really boggles their minds: When they observe, or photograph, electrons, they find that this act can change their speed and behavior.

Physicists find this subatomic world not only puzzling and maddening but also shocking. Einstein never accepted subatomic findings. Erwin

Schrodinger, an early twentieth century Austrian Nobel-prize winner in theoretical physics, who was in on early discoveries in quantum physics, said: "I do not like it. I am sorry I ever had anything to do with it." Quantum physicists now know a lot more than they did say, 75, 25, or even one year ago. But from early on they have contended that, along with the unimaginable size of the universe, the smallness and unpredictable antics of the subatomic world are realities that our *Homo sapiens* brain does not and perhaps cannot, grasp. Nobel prize-winning, quantum physicist, Richard Feynman said, "I think I can safely say that no one understands quantum mechanics." With the discovery of this dynamic, minuscule world, we must face the fact that reality is not as it appears to be, even to scientists with their highly sophisticated instruments. And many scientists now doubt that we are intelligent enough to figure out the universe.

Despite our confusion about this world of exotic, tiny things, knowledge of it has made possible such beneficial marvels as the silicon computer chip, lasers, the electronic microscope, and magnetic resonance imaging (MRI). Most importantly, it shattered and made scientists abandon the centuries-old idea of a universe governed only by law. Because of quantum physics, we now see that the universe is a single, unified system. It is made up not only of laws and predictability but also of interactive and entangled energies that produce random events, surprises, contradictions, chance, unpredictability, or what scientists call *indeterminability*, and even occasional chaos.

Scientists still assume that law and order in nature are real—indeed, it's because of them that chaos and *indeterminability* mean anything. But laws we can count on, for all practical purposes, now pertain only to macro space, the parts of reality you and I live amidst and connect to through our five senses. Interestingly, the observation that the universe operates by surprise as well as law implies that reality has dimensions of openness. This suggests to me that it may have space for the activity of spirit. It's this openness that has mystics exploring the material cosmos and scientists writing sonnets about the wonders they encounter in the natural realm.

I noted earlier that, because we are now aware of the staggering size of the universe, our knowledge poses profound problems for supernatural religion based on the ancient heaven-up-there, hell-down-there model. I'm now saying that the quantum realities at which we've just looked pose grave challenges to scientists still wedded to a universe governed totally by law. Most scientists consider quantum realities the key to unlock our scientific future. We'll look at the implications of this in the next two chapters.

Everything Evolves

Where did everything come from? The current scientific worldview claims that some 13.7 billion years ago, an incomprehensibly dense, heavy, small particle, in the tiniest fraction of a second, exploded and blew into existence our material universe. Scientists call this explosion that started it all the Big Bang. From their gaseous beginnings, the stars and planets and everything else that fills the immensity of space, including, as of late, us humans on planet earth, have evolved, or developed, over a long period of time. What existed in the way of space-time before the Big Bang? Nobody knows. Why did it happen when it did? Nobody knows. But everything science knows today points to something like the Big Bang to explain the creation of the universe a little short of 14 billion years in the past. By our standards of time, that's a long, long time ago.

Through most of the last three decades of the twentieth century, David Cudaback was an award-winning astrophysicist on the faculty of the University of California, Berkeley. He also was active in the life of the Montclair Presbyterian Church in the hills of Oakland, where I was pastor most of that time. His wife, Dorothea, also a U.C. professor and Family Development Specialist, was a church member. Dave playfully referred to himself as our "resident atheist," though, actually, he was one among several. Everyone loved him. He celebrated with us, was involved in our art and environmental projects, and led us to the university's famous Lawrence Hall of Science and on nighttime hikes to observe glorious meteor showers.

Sometime in the early 1990s, I asked Dave if he would be willing to explain the Big Bang to those in the church family who would like to hear it from a real scientist, and he said yes. So one evening, about 25 of us gathered to hear him outline the theory in some detail. Before we began our follow-up discussion as a group, Dave summarized the theory in rather dramatic terms. He pointed out again that all the matter in the universe was once crammed into a dense, tiny sphere, smaller than a pinpoint, and that it then, inexplicably, exploded to create what has over eons evolved into the 125 billion or so galaxies we know of today.

We all sat silent, awed by his explanation. Finally, John Hadsell, our staff Theologian in Residence, raised his hand and said quietly, with a wry little smile, "*Gee, Dave, isn't it easier to believe in God than that?*" Everyone laughed, including Dave. But as far as I know, none of those secularized church people—all of whom were aware of the Bible's creation story—gave up on the Big Bang and evolution as the best explanation for how the physical universe came to be where it is right now.

But where did we humans come from? In Darwin's 1872 *The Origin of Species*, he declares that animal life, of which we are a part, evolved from the lowest to the highest forms, through an extravagant reproductive process that took place over not thousands but millions of years. The fact that some original species are still here simply means that they avoided extinction by developing the right adaptations to threats from enemies and such natural catastrophes as meteorite collisions, epidemic diseases and ice ages. In one sense, they survived by luck.

Look with me now at a time-line of critical epochs from the beginning. Scientists gain knowledge all the time. But, in regularly fine-tuning their time-lines, they do so without apology, using estimates back in time that are rounded off by billions, millions, and then thousands of years. In 2013, the time-line from the Big Bang to the emergence of human history—which stuns my mind and takes my breath away—looked something like this:

13.7 billion years ago: The Big Bang; everything begins.
4.55 billion years ago: Our solar system starts to form.
600-700 million years ago: Simple forms of animal life appear.
5-7 million years ago: Hominoids, our earliest ancestors, arrive.
200 thousand years ago: *Homo sapiens* begin taking shape.
10 thousand years ago: Civilization forms and organizes.
5 thousand years ago: We start to keep records of our histories.

Scientists estimate that since life first appeared on this planet, 98 percent of the species that ever existed are now extinct—and that reminds us that death surely is built into the pattern of life. It is good to keep in mind, too, that scientists draw these conclusions not from mindless speculation, but from sophisticated tests and extensive explorations conducted worldwide with state-of-the-art technologies.

Here is an impressive fact: Since Darwin first proposed biological evolution, no one has found one shred of evidence to contradict its basic outlines. Philosopher Daniel Dennett claims that Darwin's evolution by natural selection is "the single greatest idea any one person has ever had." And because of remarkable findings over the past century in geology, chemistry, biology, genetics and cosmology, the scientific community stands by evolution as the essential truth about the origin and nature of everything, including us.

Science also dominates how we think today, and it is scientists to whom we look to help us create a sustainable future for our planet and our personal lives. Even devoutly religious people with cancer are more eager to hear good news from their oncologist (a scientist), than from their pastor, rabbi, or imam. For now, let me suggest that if your worldview doesn't respectfully consider the Big Bang, the evolutionary time-line and the zany, mind-blowing cosmic and subatomic worlds to which science has introduced us, it needs radical readjustment.

Am I saying science is perfect? No. Should we give science our absolute trust and uncritical loyalty? Not for a moment. If scientists admonish us to question everything, does that include science? Responsible scientists say it does. I do, too. And that takes us to the next chapter.

PART THREE
SORTING OUT THE ISSUES

Any account of science which does not explicitly describe it as something we believe in is essentially incomplete and a false pretense. It amounts to a claim that science is essentially different from and superior to all human beliefs that are not scientific statements—and this is untrue.

Richard Rhodes

I believe that a scientist looking at nonscientific problems is just as dumb as the next guy.

Physicist Richard P. Feynman

An abundance of mystery is simply part of the bargain—which doesn't strike me as something to lament. Accepting the essential inscrutability of existence, in any case, is surely preferable to its opposite: capitulating to the tyranny of intransigent belief.

Jon Krakauer

Acceptance without proof is the fundamental characteristic of Western religion; rejection without proof is the fundamental characteristic of Western science.

Gary Zukav

CHAPTER 9:

THE BATTLES OF SCIENCE

Enemies Confront Science

I appreciate the light that science has shed on our universe and our nature. I also join the vast majority of Americans who are deeply grateful for the extraordinary technological benefits scientists have given us in this new age. But when science answers our first question as to where everything came from, and how it got here, despite its accumulation of massive evidence to support its claims, it gets little or no respect from about half of American adults.

Christian fundamentalists despise scientists for insisting we live in a godless universe. They counter scientists with what they call *creationism*. It's the notion I reviewed earlier that, based on the Bible's Book of Genesis, claims a supernatural God created the universe out of nothing, six to ten thousand years ago. Scientists call this idea unfounded fiction, an opinion I share. Creationists strike back at science, assailing the Big Bang and the bedrock theory of evolution. They call evolution mistaken speculation at best and "demonic deception" at worst.

Science also faces challenges from a small, more sophisticated, vocal group of believers who call their view *intelligent design* (ID). Its advocates accept much of evolution but suggest that beauty and order in nature seem built-in, which most scientists accept. But ID also holds that natural selection doesn't adequately explain the complex design in the universe, and that our world could not have emerged simply from atoms casually hurled together.

ID also insists that the "six fundamental, finely-tuned constants" that make this planet perfectly fit for the emergence of life could not have happened by sheer chance, even given an infinite number of planets. They raise that old question: Is it reasonable to assume that at least one of an infinite number of monkeys, over, say five billion years (pretend they were here that long ago), each banging away on its own word processor, would by today actually have typed a Shakespearean sonnet? Their answer is, *No!* They contend that just as we rightly assume Shakespeare's writings were not accidental but designed, it's most reasonable to conclude that things in nature that look as if they've been designed are not the product of accident but in fact the product of design. In the end, they say that for science to be true to itself, it must leave room for the possibility that the universe was created by something like a purposeful mind.

Scientists will have none of it. They contend that the arguments for ID have not held up, and they look on it as a corruption of science. Armed with fossil studies and advanced tools such as Carbon-14 and argon-argon dating, plus a map of the DNA code, they insist that evolution is not what people untrained in science think of as a *theory,* that is, someone's fanciful conjecture, or a best guess. Rather, it's an explanation of a physical reality based on repeated testing, peer review and massive, indisputable, circumstantial evidence. They claim that in applying their scientific method to nature, including our human nature, they have not found one piece of evidence that confirms the existence of a designing intelligence. Evolution, they say, is as established a theory as the theory of gravity and the germ theory of disease.

Intelligent Design advocates have focused on fighting science in public education. They try to cast doubt on evolution and pressure school boards to include the teaching of their idea in the science curriculum of schools. They charge scientists who oppose them with unfair discrimination. They argue that teachers should be required to present students with both sides in this debate. Scientists say the both-sides argument could be used to compel educators to teach the flat-earth theory alongside the scientific view that our planet is a sphere, or that demons, not germs, cause physical sickness, or the theory that the moon is made of green cheese.

It frustrates scientists that ID proponents bypass the step of submitting their data for testing, as is done in the scientific community.

Since they don't apply the scientific method to reach their conclusion, scientists do not see the controversy based in science. And having found that the institutions backing ID are rooted in Christian faith, they look on ID as creationism in disguise, as one more ploy by Christians to discredit science and put God into public education.

Scientists continue to have the upper hand with public education policy makers. But surveys tell us that as of now, early in the twenty-first century, as many adult Americans believe in creationism or ID as believe in evolution. And the efforts of ID advocates have created a chilling effect on science education, particularly in such Bible Belt states as Texas and North Carolina. It's not clear who will win this battle in the long run. People with strong convictions about their religion, and who believe their God is being "dissed," have a history of fighting tooth-and-nail against their adversaries.

This ongoing dance between science and religion drives both camps into defensive overstatement. I find it troubling that some religious leaders, and followers, shut out evidence and reason, discredit critical thinking and insist they have the truth about everything. Equally distressing, however, are scientific purists who believe they have the only to truth about all the important realities. Both can see only the false assumptions and failed reasoning of their adversaries. Sadly, these sand-box squabbles between the advocates of narrow religious and scientific views have continued well into the twenty-first century.

Friends Confront *Scientism*

By contrast, relations between scientists and progressive spiritual and religious thinkers appear warmer than in the mid-twentieth century. The cold shoulder given to religion by science began to thaw about that time. We can credit this mainly to progressive Protestant figures, who, in contrast to anti-science fundamentalists, began to concede publicly that religion does not always know what it is talking about regarding material matters.

These believers made their overtures to scientists in the wake of key medical achievements, including miracle drugs and advanced cancer treatments. They have remained impressed with science by the likes of air travel, space exploration, eyeglasses and hearing aids, electronic telescopes, television, laser surgery, computer technology, and an almost endless number of amazing products created and refined by science through the last century. They note the irony, too, that religious folk who curse science have no trouble enjoying the benefits of all the fascinating products scientists have developed.

Progressive spiritual thinkers continue to watch appreciatively as scientists apply their knowledge of the genetic code to conquer diseases, and as they map every galaxy within twelve billion light-years of Earth to better understand our universe and planet. The respect these spiritual thinkers show science makes responsible dialogue with scientists easier, though we rightly do not take amicable relations for granted.

Several problems with scientists, however, bother both the religious and nonreligious who value science. One has to do with scientific secularism, or *scientism*, the term I use in this section's title and describe in the list of worldviews in Chapter 3. I use it to tag narrow-minded secularists who, among other rigid opinions, hold that only the material is real and the scientific method is the only reliable road to truth. They insist that nothing that smacks of the spiritual is real, simply because they cannot test it with their scientific tools. In other words, they decide what true knowledge is by accepting only their own method of finding it. This strikes me as the same self-importance some religious authorities and nonreligious spiritual gurus display when they claim to know the one way to truth. Follow them and they will lead you, they say, "to Paradise!"

The highly-decorated theoretical physicist John Polkinghorne, who left his position at the University of Cambridge for the Anglican priesthood, doesn't buy *scientism*. He sees two important ways to look at reality: the scientific, and the poetic. To illustrate them, he uses the question of why a pot of water is boiling on the stove. The observing scientist answers: "The pot boils because the burner flame over which it sits is high enough and has had enough time to heat the water beyond 212 degrees Fahrenheit." That's a true, scientific explanation. But the husband of the house comes home tired from work and may care little about the science of boiling water. He tells us, "The pot is boiling because my beloved lit the burner and put the pot over it so we could enjoy a welcoming cup of tea together." That also, we know, is a true explanation.

Here is another illustration of the different ways to state what is real: First, the scientific description of a sunrise: "The earth, rotating while in orbit around the sun, turned to such a degree that it increasingly exposed us, where we happen to be, to sunlight." Until the sixteenth century, no one would have any idea of what this meant, but today we know it to be a true statement, one that corresponds to what is real.

Second, the poetic description: "The sun came up this morning." We say, "Yes, indeed it did." People always have known that this is a helpful way to note what did away with the darkness of night and brought us to daylight.

Scientific purists also reject the notion that behind the universal human yearning for meaning can lie something more than the need for relief from animal anxiety. They cannot see it as a spiritual quest to which the scientific method simply does not apply. Some scientists are looking for what they call a "God gene" to explain our profound longing for purpose, loving connections, and wholeness. Others think that our distinctive bent toward such ends is an "evolutionary adaptation," or "side-effect." Biologist and neo-atheist Richard Dawkins has called it a "neurological accident," a "mistake" in the evolutionary development of our brain.

I wonder if it is so unquestionably logical that these strong, uniquely human drives are an accident, a "virus of the mind," an "evolutionary blunder," a "biological goof." Might it not make more sense to deduce that we all have these innate longings because there are natural (not supernatural), life defining, spiritual powers working in and through us?

A related problem: scientific purists talk as if science can solve all of our problems and answer all of our questions, as if their method is foolproof as well as all-encompassing. Good scientists know that the most careful scientific minds using state-of-the-art technologies can draw wrong conclusions because of false assumptions and faulty experiments, and that scientists can be led astray by their biases and blind spots. When they rectify a mistake—which, unlike most religious leaders, they readily do and for which we must give them credit—the solution invariably raises new questions they can't answer; and every day they face more and more questions. We do well to remember that fallible people, not robots, "do" science; and that there is bad science and there are bad, even *mad* scientists. Of course, bad behavior is not unique to scientists—the same kinds of flaws typify leaders in every tough human endeavor, including politics, religion, and spirituality.

Thoughtful scientists also know that life boils down to unknowns. Most today respect the puzzles that science can't explain and are humbled by them. These puzzles pertain both to what we don't yet know and to what we do know that evokes in us, as it did in Einstein and Carl Sagan, amazement, wonder, and awe. The latest findings of the new physics, biology, astronomy, social sciences, and psychology face us in the postmodern world with much more unresolved mystery, awe, and wonder than modern science ever did. You can Google the Hubble Telescope, visit the official site, double click on the Stay Connected box and get daily e-mails that will take you on the ride of your life.

Whenever scientists insist that only the scientific method and reason lead to truth and that only the material is real, we can remind them it is they who have shown us that nature is too big, too mysterious, too unpredictable, too subtle, too flabbergasting, and too open and evasive to be captured totally. It is central to my argument that material realities do not explain everything about us, or meet all of our needs, and that the scientific method is not our only access to truth essential to our humanity.

I also suggest that the pure secular scientists are not as objective as they like to think and that their smug overconfidence in the scientific method creates just as many problems for human welfare as does unthinking religion. It's the kind of arrogance that makes you wonder which is worse: organized religion, unorganized religion, disorganized religion, magical religion, boring religion, smug religion, no religion at all, or this kind of anti-religion and anti-spirituality.

I suspect staunch, scientific secularists would deny the charge of idolatry, that is, of worshiping the material universe, reason, and the inductive method. But since they seem to give those things their adoration, absolute trust, and uncritical loyalty—the traditional marks of worship—if they don't worship them, they strike me as doing an excellent job of imitating those who do. I'm not sure what would help those who practice this cold, sometimes fanatical rationalism to see anything irrational and ironic about their worshipful behavior.

Scientists raise yet another serious problem for friends: they continue to experiment in areas that raise immense ethical questions. While eager to support good science, many nonscientists feel they must challenge the frequent failure by scientists to struggle with issues they perceive to be of moral importance. In the next chapter, we'll look at why this is necessary.

As to why we suffer the moral dimensions of our human predicament, scientists contend it is silly to believe that just a few thousand years ago a fallen angel assumed the form of a snake and seduced the first two fully grown, innocent human beings into disobeying their Creator God, and that God punished them, and us, their offspring, with a depraved nature that besets us and causes the global mess in which we find ourselves. Scientists see this account as a simpleminded fabrication. Thoughtful nonscientific people, who have not been indoctrinated by literal interpretations of Genesis, also find ludicrous the story as history.

Scientists blame our moral and ethical struggles on ignorance, superstition, fear, and anxiety. We are anxious because, even as we feel responsible for our lives, we have limited freedom and power, and all the while deep down we know that one day we will die. They also tell us our human predicament is natural; it fits an evolving, imperfect world in which death is a part of life. From the standpoint of timing, or evolution, they say we have failed to resolve our issues because our species simply has not been around long enough.

Along with religious types, scientific secularists agree that we live our best lives when we're ethical. They know that there are right and wrong, better and worse, helpful and harmful answers to ethical questions and that to survive today, we need sound ethical guidelines. And professional associations of scientists realize that we all should be held to universal standards of conduct.

Secularists believe that religious organizations should not be allowed to condone the killing of disobedient children to ward off evil spirits or placate their angry God. They think that governments ought not to imprison citizens who simply disagree with them. And they concur that scientists ought not to engage in projects that violate the dignity of fellow humans and our environment. But they tell us that to be able to do their best work, scientists must not be dictated to or disciplined by religious bodies. They insist on the right to self-regulate with their own codes of conduct. I agree that this is the ideal. But most professional scientific groups around the world are aware of the increasingly urgent need for effective global governance of science. If in the real world scientific communities fail to police themselves--as is the case with some of them--to stop scientists from running amok and putting science to evil ends, we must call on governments to enact regulations.

A central question of ethics has to do with where we get the needed guidelines. Secular scientists note that traditional religious piety, including reverence for the Ten Commandments, does not always produce noble behavior and at times seems a deterrent to it. Ironically, one might suggest they sound like the radical Jesus. In his far-famed Good Samaritan parable (Luke 10), he bluntly points out, to put it mildly, that pious people in his day lack ethical sensitivity. He has a priest and a Levite, another religious person, callously pass by a man who had been mugged by bandits and is lying wounded by the highway. Then, to rub salt in the wound of the godly, he has a godless nonbeliever, a Samaritan, respond ethically, treating the man with compassion and generosity.

Secularists also say that in a complex, changing world we need to update our ethical understandings and directives constantly. Here again, Jesus beats them to the draw in speaking to his contemporaries about the scriptural admonitions they inherited. When time and again he declares, "you have heard it said, but I say to you ..." he's telling his listeners that their dated moral codes have not led them to respectful, healthy community, and they need to be replaced. See Jesus' comments on several commandments in what we know as the Sermon on the Mount (Matthew, Chapters 5-7).

Thoughtful scientific secularists say that we must develop ethics that will benefit everyone. The good is not only what contributes to the preservation of our species but also what enhances the mental and emotional well-being of everyone. Our experience of the good, they contend, relies, in main part, on the healthy social and cultural contexts we build and the effort we put into being and doing good. We can be good, they contend, if we will obey natural law, use the scientific method to increase knowledge and sharpen our minds, and follow a common sense of decency. Many believe that if we make every effort to be sure everyone's needs are met, we can create a relatively safe, disease-free, better world for most people. Secular scientists also say that since there is no God to direct and threaten us, no God to fear or love or listen to, we must solve our own problems, we must face the predicament together and negotiate ethics to protect and enrich the common good, which, of course, is what we've been trying to do in our secular democracy.

But where do we get the will to do what is right once we know what it is? To negotiate social, political, and medical ethics that will benefit everyone strikes me as respectful of human dignity and a worthy goal. A key question is whether scientists themselves can and will submit to negotiation. They notoriously disagree not only about *what* our needs are but also about how we best can meet them. They also do not always show opponents the respect needed for constructive negotiation. As we all do, they often take the easy way out when deciding what is right, settling for the lowest common denominator and giving in to those who wield power, have the loudest voices, or offer the most money. Like the rest of us, they too often don't have the will to do what is right even when they know what it is; our moral failures are most often due not to a lack of knowledge but to a lack of courage to face the knowledge we already have. Of critical significance, some scientists insist on the right to do something scientific just because they can, no matter what the consequences. Since this particular nonethic has led to huge problems, the difficult task of defining ethics will take humility, as well as wisdom, vigilance, and persistence in negotiation, by everyone involved.

When we talk of negotiating ethics for our American community, another group presents problems. They are the *Ten Commandments* moralists who distrust science and who vote based on scripture rather than reason, but who must be included in any negotiation and voting. They already block and distort reasonable medical ethics that respect women, minorities, the poor, and the terminally ill, all based on a few words cherry-picked from various ancient scriptures.

Here's another question to ask of scientists: When you speak of building a better world, what do you envision? Is it the assembly-line, mind-controlled *brave new world* about which Aldous Huxley was warning us nearly 100 years ago? Is it a remake of the bleak and failed twentieth-century Soviet Union? Is it a society like the one we seem to be approaching, in which everyone becomes captive to digital gizmos and even the most creative work of people takes second place to robots? Or is it some other impersonal, dreary scientific dream world? I would like to hear from the various sciences about the technical, moral, and ethical world they foresee.

Scientists know that young people love the gadgets they produce: iPads, laptops, smart phones, and whatever else is new. They also are aware that while the young look to them to deliver a sustainable future, they are increasingly anxious about the apocalyptic clouds gathering on the scientific horizon. They also disdain that dark side of science and disapprove of its doing whatever it damn well pleases. In 2014, alert Americans are protesting the great scientific experiment, wherein our food companies are including inadequately-tested, unannounced *genetically engineered ingredients* in their products. Even scientists are finding the often-praised promise of science unreliable and sometimes downright scary.

The more arrogant among scientists put up formidable resistance when those who value science challenge their right to be able to do whatever they want. And even as we raise serious questions about the scientific enterprise, we must deal with a new force that tends to worship science and is impacting the American consciousness rather significantly.

The New Atheists

Early in the twenty-first century, American radar picked up strong signals from a brand new atheism rooted in an uncritical adoration of science and reason. In 2005, authors Richard Dawkins, Daniel Dennett, Sam Harris, and the late Christopher Hitchens began unleashing relentless frontal attacks on the views and violent acts of religious fundamentalists around the world. The bulldog approach of these men made a big splash on the American literary scene. Their books topped *The New York Times* and *Amazon.com* bestseller lists for longer than anyone would have predicted; their lectures generated vigorous debate on university campuses; and they enjoyed a rash of national television appearances usually reserved for rock and movie stars. Their debunking of the superstitions and fanaticism that mark much of traditional religion rang a bell with a lot of people. Their rhetoric energized longtime atheists, who felt they had suffered long enough from being off-center in a culture dominated by religion.

Like the old atheists, these new believers are pure secularists and reject anything spiritual rooted in religion. We consider their atheism new for several reasons. One is that they buttress atheism's longstanding arguments with with the latest scientific findings. Another is that, while the old atheists tended to criticize religion behind closed doors, the new atheists plead their case before the reading and television-viewing public. And in contrast to how atheists were treated in the past, a major slice of educated America has welcomed the present breed with open arms.

Atheists used to refer to themselves simply as those who lack a belief in the existence of God. By contrast, today's *disbelievers* (their term), whom we might better call *anti-theists*, attack fundamentalism for its anti-science stands, rejection of critical thinking, friendship with violence, and its oppression of minorities and women. Their ridicule is meant to undermine the American Christian right and ultra-Orthodox Jews who insist Israel deserves exclusive right to the land of Palestine because long ago God gave it to them, and Muslim extremists who seem to hate anything non-Muslim.

On the surface, the new atheists are unleashing a backlash against bad religion. Yet, they are doing more than that. A fear of fanaticism, right-wing politics and terrorism may have triggered their attacks; but their loathing of faith, *per se,* has produced their most bombastic broadsides. Religion itself, some of them declare, is evil, *poisoning everything it touches.* They would love nothing more than to wipe it from the face of the earth.

In their hatred of religion, these atheists ignore the contributions of progressive believers to the arts, democratic community, higher education, social justice, peace, human rights, medicine, and compassionate social support systems. Thoughtful nonbelievers acknowledge that those gifts deeply enrich us, even when they come from secularists who also are religious. I suggest we must chide these atheists for assuming that by ridiculing fundamentalists they invalidate the good work of serious, secular believers. Many progressive religious folk have almost as little in common with fundamentalists as do the atheists themselves.

The rhetoric of the new atheist spokespersons also raises the hackles of scientists, whom you might expect would be sympathizers. These scientists dislike the new breed of atheists for overstating their arguments; for bashing religious people with a sledgehammer rather than dissecting their beliefs surgically; for calling religion the greatest source of conflict in the world and then promoting disagreeable conflict with religion; and for declaring believers stupid and atheists smart (Dennett actually proposed that atheists dub themselves *Brights*).

Some scientists have openly charged these atheists with giving science a bad name. In particular, they've criticized Dawkins for impugning the integrity of scientists who have impeccable professional reputations but who are spiritual-friendly or affirm a religious faith of their own. Dawkins condescendingly psychoanalyzes and scorns them, accusing them of being senile, or "closet atheists" who fear they won't receive financial grants if they admit to their real persuasion. If the shoe were put on the other foot, it would be like arguing that Dawkins is caustic toward religion because it sells books.

I find it a bit ironic, too, that while atheists assail all religions, their social justice, public heroes often are persons of faith, such as Ghandi, Martin Luther King, Jr., and Bishop Tutu.

Another sad irony: the new atheists have called agnostics "cowardly atheists." Their nasty putdowns of all but their own kind tell us they ignore the ethic not to demonize those who differ with us and to present ourselves as superior or righteous. One Stan Guthrie says: "Apparently, the new atheists didn't get the tolerance memo."

Their often bitter spirit, misconceptions, rhetoric, and dogmatic and extreme responses strike me as unbecoming; and I find their critics correct about their bad behavior. Actually, they appear to me to enjoy too much being "bad boys"—referring to themselves, while smirking, as "godless unbelievers." They say, "The emperor (religion) not only has no clothes, he's also ugly." But even as they speak, their own behavior, at least at times, is far from pretty.

Having said that, I think these atheists correctly criticize fundamentalism's literal interpretations of the Bible, its fairy tale-like dogmas, its fear of critical thinking, its rigid indoctrination of children (atheists call it *brainwashing* and *child-abuse*); its doting on petty morals and the afterlife while neglecting social and economic justice; its disregard for human suffering; its ready use of violence; and its animosity toward science. I also, by the way, think the atheists rightly criticize liberal theologians for not speaking out against the lunatics and violent fanatics connected to their own faith traditions.

If you don't like the behavior of these scientific atheists or agree fully with them (as I don't), you must at least grant that, after thousands of years of ignorance and sentimental attachment to superstition, most of the last century's major advances in knowledge were achieved by scientists without the help of appealing to God and have benefited humankind in uncountable ways. We also must note that the new atheists have made no small contributions to the larger American consciousness: They have been vigilant in confronting attempts by Christian fundamentalists to make our country a theocracy; they have spurred atheists to come out of the shadows and form local groups; and they have gotten a lot of religious people to think for the first time.

Many atheists admit that science and reason alone do not address their deepest needs as persons. In their business or professional circles, like everyone else, they often face ruthless competition, petty politics, greedy manipulation, rejection, and isolation. Discovering elusive knowledge, or learning of new scientific discoveries, may fascinate them, but free inquiry and intellectual broadening takes them only so far. They also may have fun bashing religious folk and seeing themselves as more intelligent than them, but feeling superior offers little inner nourishment, communion, or real joy.

American Atheists often suffer lonely existences. This happens not only because the religious majority has ridiculed and rejected them but also because our urban society itself has suffered the loss of community. In addition, organized atheism has not offered much in the way of holidays to celebrate, or nourishing community focused on guidance for personal growth, relationships and ethics. Atheist groups that have been around for some time, therefore, have not enjoyed a reputation for their warm welcome and loving support.

As of late 2013, we catch glimpses of change. Begun in Britain, a movement has sprung up in the United States that involves the establishment of Sunday Assemblies. (Google it.) In cities across the country, nonbelievers are gathering for quiet reflection, singing and live music, inspirational talks and, in some places, stand-up comedy—all without God. Many participants once were part of organized religion and miss the sense of human connection it gave them. Now, they focus on improving themselves, building personal support relationships, helping those in need, and contributing to the larger community, not as isolated individuals but in the company and support of other freethinkers. In California, atheist groups are coming together not only to combat the Tea Party's influence but also to lobby for secular legislation. The vitality of the new atheism has spurred these atheists into a new way of life marked by "being in community."

Here's another bit of good news for those who don't look to religion and God for help but who value community and ethical guidance. The University of California at Berkeley sponsors the *Greater Good Science Center*. (Google it.) The center claims concern for *The Science of a Meaningful Life*. It offers members the opportunity to connect with others who seek "a more compassionate and resilient society." For a rich personal life, the Center stresses cultivating spiritual habits such as gratitude, forgiveness, kindness, altruism and compassion. It is an interdisciplinary research center devoted to the scientific understanding of happy and compassionate individuals, strong social bonds, and altruistic behavior. While serving the traditional tasks of a UC Berkeley research center—fostering groundbreaking scientific discoveries—the GGSC is unique in its commitment to helping people apply scientific research to their personal experience.

Give the feisty new atheists credit for some other good things: They have relocated atheism itself—perhaps for a long time to come—from the edges of American culture to the center of struggles for truth. And no matter how obnoxious they've been, it is they who have rightly taught us to challenge ancient worldviews that cannot survive unbiased scrutiny in the light of day. So if your worldview includes any kind of god, faith, or supernatural spirituality, you owe it to yourself to be familiar with what these new freethinkers are saying. You can gain this knowledge, along with cogent criticisms of their best ideas, simply by looking inside their books and reading reader reviews of them on Amazon.com, or by Googling them by name.

A long-standing liberal idea says that no one should criticize others' beliefs, no matter how bizarre or silly they are. The rule sounds reasonable and generally ought to be followed. But today, religious fundamentalists tell us that violence and fanaticism are an acceptable norm. And because our world brims with guns and WMDs, I suggest we all—progressive religious and nonreligious groups alike—set aside the general rule and, without becoming mean-spirited, join with the new atheists to expose religion that thrives on blind-faith, authoritarianism, self-righteousness, the toleration if not the use of violence, and on bigotry aimed at atheists, other believers, ethnic minorities, women, gay, lesbian, bisexual, and transgender people.

Extremists in both religion and science can be scary. We rightly challenge them. But what else is there on the secular side of things we need to be concerned about?

We have sought for firm ground and found none. The deeper we penetrate, the more restless becomes the universe; all is rushing about and vibrating in a wild dance.

Max Born

The interface between science and religion is, in a certain sense, a no-man's land. No specialized science is competent here, nor does classical theology or academic philosophy really own this territory.

Holmes Rolston, III

Science is not only compatible with spirituality; it is a profound source of spirituality. When we recognize our place in an immensity of light-years and in the passage of ages, when we grasp the intricacy, beauty, and subtlety of life, then that soaring feeling, that sense of elation and humility combined, is surely spiritual. So are our emotions in the presence of great art or music or literature, or acts of exemplary selfless courage such as those of Mohandas Gandhi or Martin Luther King, Jr. The idea that science and spirituality are somehow mutually exclusive does a disservice to both.

Carl Sagan

Science without religion is lame. Religion without science is blind.

Albert Einstein

CHAPTER 10:

ON BEING FULLY SECULAR

Scientists Check Themselves

Fortunately, over the last several decades certain factors have helped scientists check their haughtiness. For one, they recognize that some of the world's greatest scientists have been friendly to spirituality, even religion. They note that Darwin had been a "reluctant" evolutionist due to his religious upbringing. And while biographers found no evidence that, as some believers claim, he converted back to Christianity late in life, he never put religion down but assigned it a different role than that of science (Google "Darwin and religion").

Einstein was reared in Germany by Jewish secular parents but attended a Catholic school, which he liked. As an adult he rejected the God of Judaism and Christianity and was seen as an atheist. But because he saw the clockwork-like laws of the universe as "no accident," he considered himself more of a deist enamored of pantheism. He upset many of his scientific friends with the comment that when he contemplated space-time, he found himself rapt in the awe of a "cosmic religious feeling." He called scientific discovery a "profound spiritual experience," comparing it to "divine ecstasy." Like Darwin, Einstein saw scientific and spiritual geniuses cut from the cloth of faith, since both dealt with things unseen and, in the absence of proof, have sought to help human beings come to terms with critical aspects of life and to "appreciate its awesome oneness." And while never enamored of the traditional Western theistic religions, and clearly not talking about traditional faith, Einstein wrote, as noted at the beginning of the chapter: "Science without religion is lame."

Please understand that I'm not arguing for traditional religion. But I get Einstein's point: to discover new truths may enthrall scientists, and they may spend much of their lives in rapture, filled with wonder over the size, complexity, beauty and mysteries of the universe. All well and good. But their findings do not touch the profound sense of disconnection and uncertainty we as humans know in relation to one another; their experiments and calculations say nothing about the spiritual experience *agapaic* love offers and that all of us so desperately need in order to be whole.

In the past half century, internationally renowned scientists have exhibited a spiritual and even religion-friendly perspective. They include John Polkinghorne, the highly honored British theoretical physicist mentioned earlier; Arthur Peacocke, England's often decorated physical biochemist; the late Charles Townes, the 1964 Nobel Prize winner in Physics from U.C. Berkeley; Stephen Jay Gould, widely read and often quoted Harvard paleontologist; Francis S. Collins, the director of the international Human Genome Project; and Freeman Dyson, the eminent Princeton physicist. Are the vast majority of scientists religious? I suspect not. But when scientific giants like these speak positively of religious matters and of their own spiritual interests, it should be hard for fellow scientists to mock everyone who takes a similar position as ignorant or an anti-science creationist. Fortunately, increasing numbers of *true* scientists are showing both humility and honesty in their dialogues with progressive religious and spiritual leaders.

I've been hard on traditional and extreme religion, and rightly so. The medieval Church in its Crusades and the Inquisition engaged in atrocious torture, terrorism and murder. In this country today, we must deal with the still active Ku Klux Klan, whose members claim to be Bible believers, and the *Christian* American Patriots Militia, a group that says, as I write this paragraph in the fall of 2013, that based on the Bible and our Constitution they have the right to kill President Obama. And we're all aware of Islamic fanatics, who continue to wreak havoc around the world with their suicide bombings and other vicious atrocities.

But science also has a checkered history and bears shame. Even scientists critical of religion find themselves humbled by the fact that their laundry is not clean. The practice of science can be a ruthless business. Its history reveals a profession rife with petty jealousies, personal betrayals, and even bitter hatred between scientists who are jockeying for power and vying to be known for important discoveries. It tells of flagrant deceptions that include the falsification of research and the fabrication of data by scientists competing for finite funds in pursuit of hefty corporate grants or professional recognition.

It was scientists who developed toxic chemicals for flame retardants and stood by the chemical industry as it lied to the citizens and legislatures of Maine and California. They did this lying in disregard not only for the public's interest but also for its safety. Scientists also have been complicit in pharmaceutical scandals, including the use of thalidomide back in the 1950s, which caused unintended horrors in the newly born. They have put life itself in serious jeopardy with the pesticide DDT, and nuclear, biological, and chemical weapons.

Historians have brought into the open the fact that scientists have secretly used humans as guinea pigs to advance their knowledge. They have shown us that scientists were all too willing to help the villainous regimes of Hitler, Stalin, Mao, and Pol Pot carry out ghastly genocides in the mid- to late twentieth century. And today scientists acknowledge that, by making possible the internal combustion engine and the use of lead in gasoline, they have contributed to our heavy carbon footprint and climate change.

All this is not to say that science and all scientists are bad. It *is* to say that when science capitulates to greedy nationalistic ends or corrupt business powers, it can poison societies just as surely as bad religion does. Apropos of what we are talking about here, it is evidence that religion is not—as the new atheists and hard-line secularists charge—the sole cause of all the evil in the world.

I agree with scientists that religious authorities ought not to make judgments or pronouncements on matters suited to the scientific disciplines. It's particularly appalling when spokespersons for religion distort scientific facts, use pseudo-science to support anti-scientific opinions, or parade religious ideas as science. But honest scientists concede that they themselves at times have closed their minds to evidence they disliked, held too long to theories based on erroneous evidence, and rejected claims to spiritual realities on which they had little expertise. And this self-awareness makes them more humble when they converse with open-minded nonscientists.

Ever since scientists unlocked the astonishing subatomic world of quantum mechanics, that world has restrained any tendency they had toward professional conceit. They were shocked and humbled by the creative activity, mystery, paradox, and seemingly lawless unpredictability they discovered. Not too long ago, they would have scoffed at the idea of such activities, but these findings they could not ignore or deny.

In addition, many scientists who once were certain that science will one day gain full knowledge of the universe have lost that confidence. They face the disquieting fact that whenever they resolve a profound scientific question, the answer presents them with a whole new set of problematic questions. As scientists continue to solve mysteries as fast as they can they are finding new ones. True scientists agree with mid-twentieth century social critic H. L. Mencken, who wrote: "Penetrating so many secrets, we cease to believe in the unknowable. But there it sits nevertheless, calmly licking its chops."

When it comes to spiritual realities, I differ with the thinking and rhetoric of hard-core scientific materialists, including the new atheists. They insist that claims to truth be limited to those found by their technical methods and explanations. Yet, some of them believe that intelligent beings probably exist in other parts of our vast universe. Some believe that one day we may discover up to seven other dimensions in our universe beyond time and the three spatial dimensions, and that in fact an infinite number of universes may exist that are radically different from our own. I think it's a bit strange, then, that these secularists find preposterous the notion that deep in the universe and in us resides a dynamic, creative force through which human life came to experience its unique sense of dignity and purpose.

I contend that our extraordinary self-consciousness, defined and driven by *agape*, makes spirit not only credible but also critically important to our welfare and survival. I do so even as I hear materialists deny its reality. Their right to remain uncertain about the existence of a distinctive human spirit, I don't question. What I challenge is their dogmatism and smugness, which allows them to ignore consistent data and thoughtful testimony from universal human experience. They hold tightly to their negative certainty about spirit even though they cannot agree on such central issues as the relationship of the brain to the mind, what human consciousness is, and even the nature of matter—Is it atoms and molecules, interfering waves, vibrating strings, the same as energy, or what?

Again, I hope you know that I am not arguing for belief in the biblical God, or for the notion that belief in God is a virtue—I don't view believers as good and unbelievers as bad. But what annoys me is the leap of faith that some scientific secularists take to deny boldly the existence of any kind of God, or transcendent reality. They jump directly from, "We have no evidence for God," to "There is no God." I have no problem with their saying: "We don't see solid evidence for God; therefore we are not convinced God exists"—that's a rational position to respect. But we must remind those who leap from, "There is not enough evidence for God" to "Therefore, God does not exist," that wishful thinking is not the same as air-tight evidence. Ironically, scientists and atheists commonly charge those who believe in the spiritual with wishful thinking and being irresponsibly irrational.

I have long admired the late, great astrophysicist and atheist Carl Sagan. At the beginning of this chapter I quote him positively about science and spirituality, from his 1995 book, *The Demon-Haunted World: Science as a Candle in the Dark*. Earlier, in the 1980s, he famously declared while introducing his impressive *Cosmos* television series: "The universe is all that is or ever was or ever will be." In such a dogmatic statement, he gave the impression he was leaving no room for any spiritual reality or any possible change in what is real. This tells me Sagan either 1) opened his mind to some kind of spiritual reality after producing that series, or 2) he didn't mean what he said in at least one of these statements, or 3) his worldview suffered from serious internal inconsistency. I'm inclined to believe he changed his mind. His earlier *Cosmos* statement reveals the kind of philosophical bias and unscientific leap of faith I'm criticizing—drawing such an important conclusion based not on testing, concrete evidence and peer review, but on opinion. And, as scientists love to tell philosophers and theologians: "Opinion is not fact." Also, ironically, it is Sagan who also is known for saying: "Absence of evidence is not evidence of absence."

While I am not promoting faith in a supernatural God, I join those who question how thorough and unbiased the search by scientists for evidence of God has been. While most of them begrudgingly acknowledge they cannot disprove God's existence any more than anyone can prove it, their search must consider certain possibilities: Maybe God is not at all like the deity portrayed by religion, just as our universe is nothing like what ancient peoples thought it to be. Isn't it possible that God is simply too big, too close, too distant, or too hidden for our best state-of-the-art scientific instruments to detect? Maybe scientists have unwittingly been looking for God in the wrong places, or in the wrong ways. Or, perhaps they have stayed unscientifically closed-minded in seeking an ultimate, nonmaterial reality, which can in fact only be found with the open eyes of imagination.

I noted in the Introduction that I cannot cover the uncountable complex views and subtle arguments on both sides of the material/spiritual issue. I assume that readers who ever want to go further on these issues can do so through the Internet, the library or formal education. I simply am saying here that pure materialists, including the neo-atheists, often are as shortsighted, narrow-minded, biased, and mistaken as some religious thinkers.

Some progressive Jewish and Christian theologians, and some advocates of Eastern philosophies, including the Dalai Lama, are standing up against narrow materialism, even as they seek constructive dialogue with scientists who exhibit some measure of humility. These progressives refuse to defend every claim people make for religion and spirituality. Some of them do battle with anti-science fundamentalists through organizations such as Christian Clergy in Support of Religion and Science, the Network of Spiritual Progressives, and The Clergy Letter Project (Google these groups). The Clergy Letter Project actually includes three separate letters: A Christian Clergy Letter, a Rabbi Letter, and a Unitarian Universalist Clergy Letter. The signers commit themselves to support the teaching of evolution and to oppose the teaching of creationism in public schools. Many rabbis, priests and ministers, in the congregations they serve, lead an annual *Evolution Weekend* celebration close to Charles Darwin's birthday, February 12.

Secular scientists gain respect from nonscientists who see themselves as spiritual when they correct wrongs done in science's name, and remain open to responsible claims to spiritual truth. Spiritual leaders gain respect from most scientists when they affirm good science and admit to wrongs done by religion and people of faith and spirituality. And it's probably obvious that it helps relations between the groups immensely when each refrains from charging the other with causing all of the world's problems.

It's clear to me that as scientists pursue knowledge of the universe and human nature, they and spiritual thinkers focus in different ways, on different aspects of reality, asking different questions and often coming up with different answers. Many eminent leaders from both groups, however, see their disciplines connected and compatible. They believe that they share values with realistic people in disciplines other than their own, that those people have something to say to them, and that they can partner with them in developing the knowledge and compassion, the light and the warmth we need to alleviate human suffering and build a more humane world. A case in point: Renowned Harvard biologist E. O. Wilson, in his 2006 book, *The Creation: An Appeal to Save Life on Earth*, directly called on evangelicals—who are known for being heavenly minded and even anti-environmentalist—to join scientists in helping save our planet.

I'm not saying all scientists and spiritual leaders are chummy. But it strikes me that the goal is not to get science and spirituality into complete harmony; it is merely not to have them in profound, unnecessary discord. And to the degree the mutual understanding, respect and forbearance we have seen continues to grow and help both groups to become more authentically secular and spiritual, all of us will benefit.

So, here's a bit of good news: Progressive theologians, nonreligious spiritual thinkers, and professional secular scientists tend to be more open, humble and civil than they used to be. But as this informal dialogue goes on, the question remains: What does it take for you and me to be most authentically secular?

Checking Ourselves for Balance

It is clear to me that in the quest for wholeness we must drop any imbalance we have between our spiritual and secular sides. If you picture yourself above material concerns, stop and count how your life has been enriched by scientific progress in such areas as transportation, medicine, and digital communication. You also ought to be able to applaud secularists who care about human dignity and are open-minded enough not to reject the possibility of spiritual realities. You can work with others to condemn religious and spiritual hucksters who prey on the uneducated and weak, or who pit spirituality against science, or who try to impose their beliefs on others.

If by contrast you think of yourself only as a truth-seeking secular person, you can add depth and breadth to your life by honoring spiritual people who also care about truth related to the universe and who refuse to claim more for their spirituality than it deserves. You also can support those who challenge secularists who use scientific knowledge for profit at the expense of others, or for destructive and violent ends. Just as most spiritual people don't stand up to religious exploiters, most secular people I know don't bother to confront those who abuse their scientific knowledge and skills. We all can call religious people and secularists to account for such behaviors.

Robert Frost said that "we don't go on to the tennis court to see if the lines are straight but to play tennis." Let me make a related point: No matter how artfully you carry a tennis racquet, wear the clothes, memorize the rules, and check every inch of the court lines, you can't call yourself a tennis player unless you step on the court not only knowing the game but able to play it. The same goes for being fully human. To know what it takes to live your best life may distinguish you from the other species and from other humans as well; but it gives you no real title to being a whole person. Life is essentially experiential, relational and practical, and wholeness requires you not simply to hold in your head a worldview that is internally consistent and in touch with reality—no matter how important that is—but also to live the life it calls for.

Whether you've been sentimentally mushy in your spirituality, or you've been stone cold in your scientific *secularity*, you can begin acting in ways true to both your secular and spiritual sides and find a healthy balance. We are coming closer to identifying answers to our central question: What does it take to be a spiritual and secular person in our postmodern world?

Not Being Duped by Secularism

In our quest for secular maturity and spiritual fulfillment, we do well to clear out any overgrown underbrush in our brains created by uncritical thinking and the passive acceptance of tradition and superstition. We must share scientists' distrust of daft claims to experience of spiritual reality. We rightly are wary when people report they've chatted with a dead person, or been healed by an angel, or survived a deadly disaster due to God's protection, or been helped by Jesus to win a beauty contest, or been told by God to invade another country and kill its inhabitants. We must not be gullible. We also must not be lazy secularists and immediately shut down our minds to every claim to experience we don't understand and can't measure. We can make healthier responses than that. We'll look at some of those responses in a moment.

Also, we must not worship science or play into the hands of a rigid, closed-minded *secularism*. If we take everything science says without question, responsible scientists will tell us we are not being scientific, and that we do well to stop doing that. They know they are often wrong about their findings and must modify their theories. They regularly run into mystery, unpredictability and new questions their tests can't answer. The most thoughtful among them think we are not wise to accept uncritically any particular scientific report, or to believe science gives us a full account of reality, or to view all of science's achievements as progress.

Another mistake to avoid is being seduced by the widely accepted, toxic values promoted these days by those pushing a self-absorbed, hedonistic secular lifestyle. The catchwords for these values are so common in American lore they pass for normal and acceptable, even as they undermine our attempts to be authentically spiritual and secular. Here are some of the more popular formulas:

1. The more things you accumulate, the happier you will be.
2. Your true purpose is to shop, spend and consume.
3. To live fully is to grab onto as much as you can.
4. Bigger is better, with regard to your business, car, or estate.
5. To be cool, you must get the latest model of everything.
6. Life's main goal is to be smart, rich, thin, and sexy.
7. You can be all you want to be and you can have it all.
8. Business lives to turn a profit, not serve the common good.
9. To lose is an embarrassing disgraceful and unacceptable.
10. If you outdo others and win, you can esteem yourself.
11. Wealth is a sign of one's importance and worth.
12. Assuming debt past your ability to repay is okay.
13. Parents can live only for themselves or for their children.
14. Forget heroes and copy the lifestyles of celebrities.
15. Whatever are your problems, take drugs to solve them.
16. People different from you don't deserve your time.
17. Stand by your country, whether it's right or wrong.
18. To use violence to resolve conflicts is acceptable.

As one who celebrates his secular side, I find these values shallow and dangerous, betraying the best in us, paralyzing us and inhibiting our drives for a good life. I suggest that to be genuinely secular we must stare down these claims and not let them dictate who we become. I encourage you to take a pen in hand and run a line through any of these 18 ideas you will not buy into from now on.

Still another mistake is to settle simply for factual knowledge. As important as it is, it is not enough—living in today's world requires us to interpret facts in light of values and to act, for our survival is at stake. Before it's too late, as we work for better balance in our personal lives, for the sake of our children and grandchildren we must join together with others of good will to do what we can to help sustain our future Unfortunately, the interacting powers are not all in accord, and finding our way will not be easy.

Some scientists call us to respond to climate change, while others create machines that contribute to it. Some work on better ways to communicate with other nations while others build super weapons that threaten our survival. For their part, some religious people continue to ignite deadly religious and ethnic hostilities and prompt us to ignore the needs of our environment and those of other nations and religions. Secular, religious and spiritual people all share blame for the menaces of climate change and violent extremism, and all must help counter them. Each of us has knowledge, skill, energy, personal experience, political power, and cash, no matter how little, to contribute. And to make a good and lasting difference, we must commit ourselves to be authentic in both the secular and spiritual sense.

This brings us to the central question: How do we achieve such authenticity?

A Middle Way For Americans Today

I was reared in a traditional Protestant family and then trained in philosophy and theology, with a modicum of psychology. Since my formal education, I've spent more than a half century reflecting on and reading about religion's supernatural worldview and the locked-in secular worldview of science. I've found both of them wanting. Because I believe life is best based on a solid, healthy worldview, I've been building my own answers to our three big questions. I decided long ago that I will not hold to a belief simply because it was taught to me as a child, or because it is popular. I found it odd and discouraging that adults will cling to religious dogma so farfetched that a tenth grader who hasn't been brainwashed will quickly perceive it as sheer nonsense. Here are examples of the *Neanderthalian* thinking from today's fundamentalists:

- A Supernatural Being created the universe in six, 24 hour days, six to ten thousand years ago (ancient and medieval believers could hold to such a scheme, but the indisputable scientific evidence we have today makes it laughable).
- We have a right to push people off of this land because our forebears tell us God promised it to us. (and that justifies mayhem against those who were here before we arrived?)
- If a young man will martyr himself killing infidels, God will reward him in heaven with a flock of beautiful, submissive virgins (a witless claim based on no evidence whatsoever).
- An angel gave Joe Smith gold-rimmed glasses so he could read God's latest revelation, and it says that your beliefs are false. (Really? God told me your brain is frozen, and you should be ashamed of such arrogance and nonsense.)
- God helps golfers win tournaments and pitchers throw no-hitters. (Does your God really do this kind of thing while every day thousands of children are starving to death?)

With no formal scientific background to speak of, I vowed to face questions raised by new scientific knowledge. I promised myself I'd trust only spiritual and scientific claims that earn the widest consent of scientists and of all of my faculties, even as I remain curious about certain others. I resolved to take the notion of *agapaic love* most seriously, because the best in religion, great literature, the arts, and my own observations and experience had convinced my brain, and every bone in my body, that this extraordinary form of respectful love is what makes human life work right.

I worked in organized religion my entire adult life. Early on I began to find offensive the claims that God's eternal truth had been dumped out of the sky long ago on Mt. Sinai, or in Jerusalem, or in Tibet, or at Mecca, or Palmyra, New York, or anywhere else. I also found it disturbing that people addicted to traditional religions tend to ignore, without apology, the implications of the latest scientific knowledge. I spent a good bit of my ministry trying to synthesize faith and reason, religion and science, the spiritual and the secular.

I value certain insights of science, of traditional Hebrew-Christian religion and of Eastern philosophy. The longer I looked at those worldviews, however, the more I became convinced that none of them responds coherently to both our puzzling universe and our dynamic human spirit. Theology and philosophy often fail to respect our need for objective truth based on hard evidence. Hard science doesn't deliver on our profound desire for intimacy, personal support and a place in the human story with a sense of worthwhile life-purpose. In other words, neither one covers both the factual and the poetic, or the material and spiritual, dimensions of human reality. Each fails to provide us with both light and warmth.

Again, we must acknowledge that science has brought us from the darkness of ignorance to the light of knowledge about the cosmos and our origins. However, if we can no more depend on the scientific method and reason to tell us what is right and what is wrong and lead us to a better, more just and peaceful world than can revered scripture, *what can we count on?*

In the next chapter, we'll look at one attempt to answer this question, an answer that affirms both the secular and the spiritual. It outlines a middle way worldview that runs between the traditional tenets of religion and pure science, merging thoughtful secular and spiritual perspectives in behalf of depth, breadth and coherence. Through its lens, you will see the physical you, and your conscious self, as intimate sides of the single reality that is you. Your body and spirit still may appear as different aspects of who you are, but now you'll see them as you do the front and back of your hand, or the head and tail sides of a dime. My premise is this: In the same way you cannot have a hand or a dime with only one side, you cannot be a real person, if you fail to honor both sides of your humanity. I trust you will put your thinking cap on and be as critical of my middle view as I have been of the worldviews I've already covered.

I call this worldview *Secular Spirituality.*

PART FOUR
TAKING A REWARDING ROAD

Folks, it's time to evolve. That's why we're troubled. Do you know why our institutions are failing us, the church, the state, everything's failing? It's because, um – they're no longer relevant. We're supposed to keep evolving. Evolution did not end with us growing opposable thumbs. You do know that, right?

Bill Hicks

It may be that religion is dead, and if it is, we had better know it and set ourselves to try to discover other sources of moral strength before it is too late.

Pearl S. Buck

Once our relief at jettisoning an outdated piece of ideological furniture is over, we must construct something to take its place.

Sir Julian Huxley

CHAPTER 11:

SECULAR SPIRITUALITY

A Middle Way

I've coined the term *Secular Spirituality* but acknowledge my debt in understanding it to numerous traditions, original thinkers, reporters, and translators from around the world, both past and present. I chose it rather than *Secular Humanism*, which identifies a movement with which I have no formal association and which has a different focus from my own. As I noted in Chapter 1, the organizations of secular humanism work mainly to keep religion out of education and government. I happen to agree with their positions, and I could be called a secular humanist. But I have chosen a more modest goal, though one I believe is equally important. I focus on your personal worldview and its influence on your life. I stress a middle way between the extremes of stone-cold secularism and sentimental supernaturalism. It's a worldview that can satisfy the curious mind when it discerns the inadequacies of these two extreme worldviews.

You will note that sometimes I refer to *spiritual secularity* and sometimes to *secular spirituality*. I use the terms interchangeably, not only for variety, but because I am convinced that spirit and the physical are expressions of the same interdependent reality that we need to keep in a relationship of tension and balance. One drawback of employing the phrase *secular spiritualists* is that historically we have identified *spiritualists* as mystics, psychics and mediums, those who claim to have extraordinary, even exclusive spiritual gifts and powers. By contrast, I am using the term to refer to ordinary people like you and me who, in our worldviews, our values and our behaviors, show respect for ourselves as secular/spiritual beings concerned about wholeness.

I know I oversimplify my description of the Spiritual Secularist worldview, and that not all Spiritual Secularists will hold to everything I include in it. Most of us have interacted to some degree with science, religion and philosophy. We draw insights from those disciplines that we believe reflect important truths. We also challenge these disciplines when they ignore important realities that an adequate worldview must address. As we Spiritual Secularists do our own thinking, we may start from different places and follow somewhat different maps, but we tend to share the same values and goals and view one another as fellow travelers along life's open road.

To best grasp what Spiritual Secularists believe are central to a thoughtful, honest worldview, we look at how they answer our three big questions: *Where did everything come from? Why is life such a predicament? How can I live my best possible life?*

Where Everything Came From

Spiritual Secularists are familiar with the popular, biblical accounts of origins in the book of Genesis. The writings describe a supernatural, tribal Sky God, who *spoke* into being everything that is. With thoughtful scientists—whom we see as fellow seekers after truth—we find loyalty to such an idea of God indefensible today. We not only lack credible evidence for such a God but, were he to exist, because of the bizarre and immoral actions He took, according to the Bible, we would deem Him unworthy of our loyalty.

We affirm the scientific findings that tell us the material universe resulted from what scientists call the Big Bang and the natural process of evolution. We see it as the most sensible explanation of how everything came to be. We believe that what science has learned about us and the size, structure and nature of the universe, demands new ways of thinking about everything, by everyone, including scientists.

We find spiritually satisfying evolution's unfolding in a pattern of emerging complexity. Unlike pure materialists, however, we don't think evolution explains everything. Even as we affirm the scientific worldview, we hold to a transforming, spiritual energy related to, perhaps even active in both biological and cultural evolution. As noted earlier, we see the purely materialistic take on reality as too spare, too narrow, too dry, and too limited to capture the breadth and depth of our astounding experiences as *Homo sapiens*.

The method and knowledge of science can unify us. Scientists do differ on method and conclusions of their investigations, but one of the strengths of science, unlike religions, is that its evidence over time tends to bring the human family together. Jews, Christians, Muslims and Buddhists all live by the same mathematics, physical laws and chemistry. These powers don't create tribes and enmity between peoples. And as over against divisive dogma, the *agapaic* love we Spiritual Secularists connect with cultural evolution can hold together, direct and inspire not only our personal lives but also the whole human enterprise. We all believe that everyone on the face of the Earth is born to grow up in all facets of our humanity, and that we cannot separate personal growth from our ability to love in an *agapaic* way. As we love, we grow and are enriched. If our love is so arrested that we cannot treat ourselves and others, even our enemies, with respect, we deteriorate to some degree from the inside out and, also, in some way we negatively affect those around us. We count the need to abide by this defining power of *agape* as the most important lesson we humans have to learn.

Please understand that when I speak of *agape*, I am not talking about an intelligent creator God, as, for example, are ID advocates. I refer simply to the evident power that defines the fullness of human relationships, grounds human ethics and calls out the best from our humanity. Exactly how this energy of *agape* relates to such events as the Big Bang, or the biological birth of life, or the cultural evolution that has brought us *Homo sapiens* to the secular reality of today, I have no real idea. As I noted earlier, while I see this question of relationship, or cause and effect, as a fascinating one, I am much more concerned to understand the significance of *agape* and how to position it and maximize it in my life.

To further identify this power at the center of our humanity, some Spiritual Secularists appeal to onetime Harvard philosopher Paul Tillich's notions of "the loving depth of existence" and "the gracious ground of all being." An important point here is that the spiritual power represented in such metaphors as "depth of existence" and "ground of being" is not separate from, outside of, or over against us. In other words, even were we to use the name *God*, we do not intend it to represent a Supernatural Being beyond space-time but rather the spiritual foundation and shaping force of *Being* itself, which includes our humanity. Some Spiritual Secularists profess to be *panentheists;* that is, they see an invigorating, life-defining force flowing in and through every living thing, without the material universe being, capturing or exhausting that force.

Along with depth and ground, some of us like to employ the scientists' subatomic term *gluons* as a metaphor for this force. In using it we are saying that *agape* is the power that not only can integrate us as persons but also can free each of us to cohere, or stick together, or form authentic community with others. Most of us think that no one metaphor or image can fully capture everything about the spiritual. I hope that whatever metaphors we use will reflect our deepest experiences of compassion, forgiveness and gratitude. Such experiences provide the warmth we so desperately need to survive and thrive. I hope too, that our metaphors will not disrespect current scientific knowledge or its method, or science's impressive track record. The steady progress of science certainly suggests that, though it may not lead us to all knowledge, it will bring to light many aspects of our humanity that we currently can't explain.

Many of us, even as we reject the notion of a *Great Father Above*, can't resist personifying the seemingly impersonal *depth*, or *ground*, or cohering *power*. We do that, not just from habit, but because the highest, most beautiful and perfect face of spirit we know is human, and personality therefore serves as an effective connecting metaphor. However, if we assign personality to *agapaic* love, we do not use, as traditional religion does, a controlling, macho-male image that demands obedience and employs the threat of punishment to get it. Instead, we employ something more like the nonsexist image of *Nurturing Parent*, the spiritual embodiment of loving support, teaching and enrichment.

One reason we see biological evolution as unable to explain everything about us goes something like this: Darwin contended that animals ferociously pursue only the knowledge they need to stay alive and reproduce. He was right about the other animals—as far as we can tell, they have no discernible interest in any other kind of knowledge. But we see him as wrong about us humans; we strive relentlessly for knowledge that has nothing to do with perpetuating our species or staying alive. A few examples: We may have needed to know simple arithmetic to insure our survival, so we evolved a brain structure that enabled us to access this mental world. Yet we insatiably pursue knowledge of complex mathematical forms, not to increase our capacity to survive, but because these forms reveal actual features of the natural world that, by their sheer beauty, excite our imaginations.

Consider, also, our craving for the arts. Think of music, in particular. We've identified its structures—harmonies, scales, rhythms and tones—and are drawn to its beauty and inspiring power, whether by Bach or the Beatles. But our thirst for understanding music, and our ability to compose, produce, dance and thrill to it, has nothing to do with helping us escape our enemies, avoid catastrophes or perpetuate our species.

Darwin's theory of knowing also doesn't account for our intimate acts of compassion, compromise and forgiveness, yet we universally hold these acts in highest honor. Brain development could have helped us learn over time that if we are good neighbors ("Love your neighbor"), we can enhance our survival prospects. But is it reasonable to believe that mere neighborliness could compel beings that are no more than biological organisms to rescue heroically from certain death a stranger or an enemy, even if it means putting their own survival at risk? Or do we know of a gene or a hormone that can override our survival instinct and liberate us to forgive those who try to kill us?

Spiritual Secularists have trouble understanding how a high moral sense could have been caused by the accidental explosions and collisions of neutrons and protons with spinning electrons, what someone has called "the blind dance of atoms." Try as we might, we don't see how *agape* could have emerged simply from the force of natural laws on bundles of physical particles. As it stands now, no one's convinced us that our incredible consciousness and dignified self-awareness are totally the product of genes, chemical action and impulses in our brain.

We contend that science has brought us great *light* regarding how the universe and human nature have been formed. But we also note that it was not Darwin or the rationalists or the new atheists who taught us that only *agape* will provide us the warmth we so desperately need to live rich and real lives; we learned this from artists, poets, and mystics, and from such diverse spiritual teachers as Lao Tze, the Buddha, the Hebrew prophets, and Jesus.

Is *agape* related to biological evolution? Here again, we don't know. Some of us think it may have been working within, under, through, or alongside the eons-long evolutionary process, as some sort of "cosmic, creative life-force." Can we explain or prove this? Not really. Even so, it strikes us as short sighted, ironic and self-contradictory for rational scientists to insist that a nonrational—actually a mindless—evolutionary process is what produced our consciousness, all the while contending that reason is the only mental process that leads to truth.

Without saying that the spiritual power of *agape* is the creator of either biological or cultural evolution, some of us see possible ways it might relate to both. We note that as more complex forms emerge in the evolutionary process, scientists say they are not a compilation of what came before. So, even when we have knowledge of the past we cannot always predict where evolution is going. Some suggest that in this open space between *what is* and *what is becoming* there may be room for a spiritual, life-defining reality to have emerged—as life itself emerged—and to be at work in human development.

Further, given that material evolution operates not only without conscious direction but also, at the micro level, by chance, randomness, and unpredictable potential, might it be that a "zone of freedom" is woven into the universe and reaches a qualitatively different level in human reality? Is it possible that, in the deep down zone of nonlaw, spirit penetrates our humanity and liberates us to rise above our animal nature and consciously join and mimic the universe's ongoing creative dance that author Barry Wood calls *The Magnificent Frolic?* Religious believers hold that their supernatural God is the choreographer of this dance. Spiritual Secularists might see it led by the nonmaterial, vital spirit, of *agape*, which they are convinced is the defining heartbeat of our human nature and unique life of responsible freedom.

Where did everything come from? The major religions contend that all things exist because a supernatural Almighty God created them. Spiritual Secularists don't believe an omnipotent, or all-powerful creator God theologians have created exists, and they find the idea of one makes no sense. If you look carefully into the Hebrew Bible, by the way, you find that the creator God was quite human: He made mistakes, failed, changed his mind To support our view, we might cite what philosophers call the *omnipotence paradox*. Here is a process of reasoning from self-contradiction that must hold true even for traditional religious believers who are threatened by the notion that their God is limited. Age-old examples of this reasoning come readily to mind:

> *God cannot exist and not exist, all at the same time;*
> *God cannot choose to violate God's own nature;*
> *God cannot build a rock so big that God can't lift it.*

I suggest that, if God is limited by such self-contradiction, the notion of *almighty* simply doesn't wash. The argument that a creator, all-powerful God cannot exist, however, has more to it than self-contradiction.

Most everyone acknowledges three momentous happenings in the history of what is. All of them deny the possibility of an "all-powerful God." The first happening is the start of the *space-time* Einstein made us aware of, and the appearance of the material universe, which science attributes to the Big Bang. Spiritual Secularists agree that the power of a universe that continues to create itself by "unbending laws" such as gravity, motion, and centripetal force limits the freedom and power of any kind of God. No matter how fervently believers trust in their God, they know they cannot jump off of skyscrapers and expect God to help them land unharmed. Once a bullet fires in the chamber of a gun and starts down the barrel, the most powerful and loving God cannot stop it, even if that God knows it's on a direct path to destroy the brain of a darling little Christian (or Jewish, or Muslim) girl. And that holds even if the whole world is praying for her.

The second major happening that limits any God is the appearance of life, for with life came death. Some scientists, by the way, think that because consciousness exists it must have been in existence from the beginning of things and may be present in every bit of matter from the stars down to quarks and neutrinos. Maybe. But the point to be made here is that, no matter when consciousness began, it came with suffering and death, much of which is senseless or serves no good purpose—except, one could argue, to save the Earth from overpopulation by its biological species. Actually, scientific findings tell us that during the past 600-700 million years, life has expressed itself in untold millions of species. Almost all of them led dreary lives and did nothing more than try to survive and are now, often after much suffering and dying, extinct. It's also clear that no God can stop any member of any species, including ours, from dying.

Finally, after the emergence of the material universe and life, evolution produced a third *Big Bang*: the shocking and relatively sudden emergence of *Homo sapiens*. This breakthrough to a radically different kind of conscious life limits any God. We are the species whose consciousness includes not only self-awareness but also moral responsibility based on freedom. Our freedom limits not only every person who relates to us but any God whom believers want to make omnipotent. Our consciousness gives us the spectacular ability to limit any God, any Great Spirit, any Ground of Being—whoever, or whatever power we might believe created us, including biological evolution that has been altered and, indeed, limited, therefore, by cultural evolution. We look on evolution as if, biologically, it had been on a fairly steady, purposeful course to formulate such a spiritual consciousness as ours, and then we emerged. Spiritual Secularists think this third, awesome breakthrough to spirit generated by *agape* is as astounding as the first Big Bang and the beginning of life itself.

So let me be clear: When we identify *agape* with the spiritual force that makes us persons and not just animals, we are not suggesting this love is all-powerful. Perfect love is limited. We do not mean it is weak and unworthy of our praise and loyalty; it's the power that can save us from despair and make us most human and joyful. It's also the reality that not only prompts us to be responsible in our relationships but also beckons us to work for a sustainable future. It's the power that prods nations, religions, races, and genders to respect one another and to erase the lines between them, paving the way for worldwide peace.

I have noted all along that at the heart of our existence are mysteries. I also have implied I join those who believe it is important that we unravel their layers. For the past several centuries, thanks to science, we have been doing an impressive job of that; and by doing so we have improved human life in many ways. For our potential benefit, we must keep pushing back the edges of significant mysteries, even with no promise that we'll be able to do it, or that it will prove to be good. But to solve all the great mysteries of which we are aware is not the primary goal for our humanity. We may never know exactly how matter and energy relate, what consciousness is and how it ties to our brain, how *agape*, if in any way, connects to evolution, or, for that matter, which did come first, the chicken or the egg. And not knowing will not be catastrophic. Our most critical human task is not to find irrefutably answer to such questions but to respect our best judicial sentiments and caring instincts, to generate the genuine warmth we need as a species, and to wisely, ethically and freely work our way through the predicament to a just and peaceful world.

Why Life is Such a Predicament

We see that disease, suffering, evil and death, and our inability to effectively counter them are mainly what the predicament is about. And we have different understandings about why they beset us so. When trying to explain why those suffering contagious diseases expose them to others, fanatics crash airplanes into skyscrapers or normally decent soldiers torture prisoners, Spiritual Secularists once again sound like the scientists. They trace evil not to the whispers of a snake or to supernatural, demonic agents but to genetic makeup, chemical imbalances, brain tumors, ignorance, irrational fears, compulsive drives from traumatic experiences when young, addictions, and to the anxiety we suffer because we know we are on a terrifying collision course with our own deaths. These inner realities create in us a compulsive, strident selfishness often too powerful to control by education, rational argument, therapy, or the threat of punishment by religion or government. One way of looking at the predicament, science says, is to see that we simply have not evolved as a species to the point we all can be reasonable and responsible.

When people engage in destructive behavioral due to the kinds of powers I've just listed, can we hold them responsible? The pure scientific secularists say, no—these humans cannot help themselves. Free will is an illusion. Genes, hormones, chemicals in the brain, plus damaged psyches determine how we act. This scientific view dominates child-rearing theory today and has all but eliminated spanking. It also designs our educational and criminal justice systems. As a result, we often let both children and adults off the hook for bad behavior. In its most extreme form, this scientific view says you have no control whatever over your actions and cannot be held responsible for them, paving the way for, among other judgments, what we call "the abuse excuse."

When American society must deal with malevolent behavior, it struggles with the tension created by this scientific view and the Puritan one that insists we all have free will and must be held accountable. In times past, under this Puritan view, bad behaviors were called immoral, even criminal, and were punished by religious or political authorities. Supporters of Puritanism say that we are less safe today because of our failure to punish. But our history is replete with stories of people who were punished severely for doing a minor wrong and who were threatened and even terrorized for believing or saying the wrong thing. Spiritual Secularists believe that some people cannot help acting in ways that damage both themselves and other, and they hold both these behaviors and such punishments in contempt. We also believe that we must limit conduct and hold everyone accountable to the law. We do well to protect our citizenry from our most perverse behaviors and, at the same time, to offer appropriate counseling and rehabilitation to those who've gotten out of control.

When we stop to reflect on the Holocaust and such dreadful genocides as those in the Soviet Union, Rwanda, and Darfur, we note that ordinarily decent citizens often become complicit in their governments' despicable acts. Such behavior shows us that civility is only skin deep, that the capacity for brutality lurks within us all and that, given certain circumstances, especially when we're convinced we must follow orders to be faithful to our God or patriotic, we all are capable of horrific, unspeakable evil.

We also should note that the predicament persists in part because *agape* is self-limiting. For the sake of guiding and protecting children, you can have parental power over them and genuinely love them at the same time. But you cannot love and attempt to control other adults— the two powers limit and even cancel each other in adult-to-adult relations. Just so, love cannot force you and me to do the right thing; it only can lure, coax and try to persuade us to that end. *Agape's* heart may break, so to speak, when we allow thousands of children to die every day of preventable hunger, disease and senseless violence, but it is powerless to stop by force our apathy and greed that contribute to those deaths.

At the same time, we see that nature has no guiding moral sense, or conscience. Tornadoes, monsoons, hurricanes, earthquakes and their tsunamis kill masses of people who happen to be in their way. Neither God, Mother Nature, nor *agape* can stop them. But even as we cite the limitations of love and nature's lack of concern for human suffering, we cannot throw up our hands. Because of what love has done to us, as Spiritual Secularists, we know we have the power to enrich the human family; minimize suffering and spread joy. We have reason to care. We are capable of caring deeply. And Eliezer Yudkowsky, whom I quote on the page before this chapter, says that we *do* care. We Spiritual Secularists see caring surface everywhere in times of serious crises and try to show our own care in a variety of ways. We want our hands to be the hands of *agape* on an everyday basis.

We know also that we make our predicament worse and shortchange ourselves when we try to settle differences by ratcheting up violence. In other words, we help create our own *hell* here and now. Of course, violence today takes on greater significance, because guns are so readily available and WMDs make a handful of disturbed terrorists capable of more monstrous atrocities than all the genocides we've ever known, put together.

How We Can Live Our Best Possible Lives

Spiritual Secularists contend that to accomplish personal wholeness and a good life we must be moral and ethical. When we act respectfully in our relations with others and contribute to the common good, we enrich ourselves internally.

But how do we know what the good is in our multicultural, ever-changing, technological world? In times past, the West drew direction from the Bible. Spiritual Secularists find that ancient moral codes, such as those in the Bible, do not provide clear-cut ethical guidance for today. The biblical books of Exodus, Leviticus and Deuteronomy lay out the laws Moses said that his God gave him on Mt. Sinai. In these writings, God condones and orders appalling ethical behavior, including keeping slaves, and stoning to death those who don't believe in Him, along with blasphemers, adulterous women, homosexuals, and those caught working on the Sabbath. We view these codes as immoral, unethical directives of a controlling, jealous, tribal God.

Some Americans, religious or not, insist that we simply need the Ten Commandments (Exodus 20). Some push to have them made visible on public property throughout the land. Again, we affirm the first commandment, not to worship idols—it is silly and beneath human dignity to give *absolute* trust and loyalty to something you make, something of *relative* value. Also, we know that the Ten Commandments include a few common-sense morals, such as don't murder, steal, commit adultery, or tell lies to violate others. But everyone knows these behaviors are wrong, and all civilized peoples in some form build them into the moral fabric of their societies. In any case, these commandments fall short because, while they tell us bad acts we ought not to do, they don't identify for us the good.

While we see ancient codes of conduct as essentially irrelevant and sometimes evil, we also find in scriptures the Golden Rule, that powerful, timeless and universal principle rooted in a*gape*: *Treat others the way you want them to treat you.* When Jesus uttered it (Matthew 7:12), he added that these few words summed up the law and the prophets for the ancient Hebrews. This ethical principle of mutual respect appears not just in the writings of Judaism and Christianity but in those of all the world's major religions and philosophies. And we all know, personally, the power this golden principle possesses--if we ignore it and cheat on a loved one, rip off a client, or lie to take advantage of someone, our spirit shrivels and something in us dies. So, down inside we know we are wise not to behave in ways that offend mutual respect.

Unfortunately, many cultures, including ours, have forgotten, lost or simply given lip service to this principle. In addition, even as we try to make out what it might mean to us, our lives are beset by constant change, competing traditions, new knowledge, hard-nosed competition, peer pressure, and ethical dilemmas. Despite the confusion presented by these realities, we all know that--even when others mistreat us--if we follow this principle and treat ourselves and everyone we meet with respect, our actions sooner or later will reward us with inner riches. Whatever parenting means, it at the least calls us to teach our offspring this ethic of mutual respect.

It is important to keep in mind that we do not strive to be ethical in isolation. We are members of communities, a democratic nation and the human family. So, to live our best lives we must be concerned with more than our own individual behavior. In our democracy we all are responsible for how our representatives at all levels of government do the right thing and work for the common good. In 2014, sadly, we lag behind many other countries in terms of income and wealth inequality, the percentage of our people living in poverty, and how we treat our children. Also, more and more people find our democracy dysfunctional and are giving up on the political process; they look to Washington for governance and get gridlock. But giving up is not an option for Spiritual Secularists. So we listen, we try to keep abreast of how our representatives are using power, we reason, we argue, we vote, we organize, we petition, we protest, and we support those who are trying their best to serve the common good.

To put our own national house in order and solve our toughest ethical problems, we must employ not only the golden principle but also the best knowledge available, our noteworthy analytical abilities, the wisdom left to us by the sages, the remarkable communication technologies at our disposal, and our highest skills in proactive diplomacy. We may distrust the ability of religion or reason alone to resolve our domestic, ethical issues, but we can draw on the best that each can offer.

We believe the Golden Rule also has profound implications for us as a nation among nations. As a positive force, it calls the United States to treat all governments with respect, including our enemies. It appeals to our best sense of what is fair, asks us to engage the best thinking from East and West, and prods us to initiate respectful international dialogue. We cannot exploit other countries, use violence as a way to resolve conflict and insist we always get our way and, at the same time, be ethical, secure, respected, and proud as a people.

In our volatile cyberspace world, not only are nations on edge with other nations, but we as a species face self-generated, daunting threats to our very survival. As the world continues to shrink, Spiritual Secularists support those who call all nations to develop a global ethic of mutual commitment aimed at securing a sustainable, just and peaceful future. We believe our government, as the major world power, bears a special obligation to get all governments to develop such an ethic. Our international sensitivity to what is unfair can help us identify the wrong. *Agape* and the golden principle can help us come closest to what is right and will compel us to do it, even if it means breaking old rules, establishing new ground and getting all nations to give up some of their sovereignty.

We all know this is no easy task. We all decry the weaknesses of the United Nations. But can we imagine a world without it? And because of it and other alliances, the world has shown signs of evolving toward maturity. We have done away with human sacrifice and cannibalism, made strides to eliminate slavery, imperialism and patriarchy, cut back on dictatorships and increased democracies, formed worldwide alliances to reduce the number of wars and weapons of mass destruction, and we are doing a better job of protecting human rights worldwide. And our own government has persuaded most nations to align with us against international terrorism. But even if we had no moral gains to celebrate, we Spiritual Secularists join those who remain faithful to the vision of a world that is more just and peaceful.

Despite these wonderful gains, we are not giddy optimists. We're aware that abject poverty still afflicts more than a billion members of the human family, that infant mortality rates remain persistently high, that war is still an option for many regimes, that crime is rampant on the Internet, and that we face looming energy and environmental crises. We also know that progress is woefully slow, particularly with regard to controlling population growth. Yes, our technological resources for meeting such crises are greater than ever. But we who pursue a better world face not only depraved worldly powers but also our own base desires, blind spots, weaknesses, and fears.

In facing the *predicament*, Spiritual Secularist draw on a variety of religious and nonreligious traditions, including the ones in which we were reared. No matter our backgrounds or associations, we generally feel good about blending insights from science and different cultural, philosophical and religious traditions. And as we try to make as much sense out of our common human existence as we can, we commit ourselves to be faithful to our vision of a world in which all have the opportunity to live their best possible lives.

Because of the prominence in American life of Christian churches, the next question to address is this: How do Spiritual Secularists with a background in Christianity, or with some abiding orientation to it, relate to the problems this tradition presents?

We'll answer this question in the next chapter.

One of the greatest challenges facing civilization in the twenty-first century is for human beings to learn to speak about their deepest personal concerns—about ethics, spiritual experience, and the inevitability of human suffering—in ways that are not flagrantly irrational.

Sam Harris

The only time my prayers are never answered is when I'm playing golf.

Billy Graham

To recover a spiritual tradition in which creation, and the study of creation matters would be to inaugurate new possibilities between spirituality and science that would shape the paradigms for culture, its institution, and its people.

Matthew Fox

Imagine there's no Heaven; it's easy if you try;
No hell below us, above us only sky.

John Lennon

CHAPTER 12:

SECULAR SPIRITUALITY VS. CHRISTIAN TRADITIONALISM

In the preceding chapter we looked at Secular Spirituality through the prism of our three basic questions. I showed you how the answers of Spiritual Secularists differ from those offered by the Western religions.

American Spiritual Secularists come from various backgrounds. Many claim no association with organized religion. Those who do are not defensive apologists for inherited doctrines about God, or for any theological party line. We simply maintain there are clues to wholeness in religion and affiliate in some way with the likes of socially engaged Buddhism, Reform Judaism and the Jewish Renewal movement, moderate Islam, Unitarian Universalism, and, in Christianity, with post-Vatican II Catholicism or progressive Protestantism.

Most of us have some sort of ongoing relationship with Christianity through one church or another or some informal expression of Christianity. What may surprise church people is that in worldview, many active clergy are Spiritual Secularists. The vast majority of them, of course, are closeted for the fear of upsetting parishioners or losing their work of ministry to which they are committed and upon which they depend for their livelihood.

I dedicate this chapter to understanding how in the world Spiritual Secularists—among whom I count myself—can remain attached to the Church and not capitulate to Christian traditionalism, a loyalty to the Church no matter what it is, says or does. If you have a strong affiliation with the Church and what you have read so far has not bothered or angered you, this chapter may do it. We'll approach the subject by examining some of the traditional Church's eccentric, superstitious, vulgar, and disgraceful teachings and practices that offend Spiritual Secularists. We start with its approach to scripture.

Christian Traditionalism Worships/Idolizes the Bible

Christians, along with Jews and Muslims, refer to themselves as *People of the Book*. Each religion sees scripture as its ultimate source of spiritual guidance and inspiration, its authority for "faith and practice." Some worship their book.

Ironically, from the Bible's perspective, the granddaddy of all sins is idolatry, not murder or stealing, or lying, or sexual misconduct. The very first of God's Ten Commandments (Exodus 20:3) tells the ancient Jews not to put another god before their God, who created all that is and who lovingly delivered them from slavery in Egypt. He outlaws their worship of a statue or image they would make of angels or demons or anything on earth or from the sea. He admits that He is a jealous God and, because of what He's done for them, He thinks He alone deserves their worship, love, and obedience. He is saying that His people shall not give uncritical loyalty to, or place their absolute trust in, anything of relative value—which means, in effect, anything or anyone other than Himself.

Spiritual Secularists charge fundamentalists and evangelicals with breaking the first commandment with their worship of the Bible. They say they love *God's Word*. We say their *uncritical adoration* and *absolute trust* amounts to idolatry.

It's not that we believe the Bible is useless. Most of us would hold that it contains some very important truths. We may believe that, if a passage gets you to be more compassionate, honest, courageous, just, or nonviolent, then, for you, it *becomes* a transforming truth and is, to you, the word of God—or of spirit, or of *agape*. But we do not see the Bible as eternal, or without error. We do not think it came down from the clouds, as anything that truly was God's Word would have had to do. We think the scriptures were written in prescientific times by men who were driven to defend their primitive impressions of what is true about our universe and human life … and some of them, at some points, sometimes got it right.

Those who idolize the Bible interpret it literally and tend to pay little or no attention to cultural context. Clergy and devout laypersons of this ilk see themselves as God's defenders. They quote scripture to pound nonbelievers into submission, and this includes their own family members and friends. Bible lovers have used scripture to justify slavery, imperialism, preemptive war, ethnic cleansing, hatred of those with whom they differ, anti-Semitism, and the abuse of women, racial minorities, and homosexuals. Our Bible-quoting Ku Klux Klan and other right-wing fanatics have created mayhem and atrocities in the name of what they believe God's Word has told them to do.

If we Spiritual Secularists pay any attention to the Bible at all, we say, along with progressive church people, that we take it "seriously but not literally." We interpret each literary form on its own terms, whether history, law, myth, saga, allegory, moral code, chronicle, census report, poetry, psalm, proverb, prophecy, gospel, liturgy, instructive correspondence, or apocalypse. We don't, therefore, take as history such early stories as Adam and Eve, Noah and his ark, and Jonah and the big fish. We believe the storytellers were trying to make a point. They intended to provide their tribe with insight into the human predicament as they saw it, giving clues as to how we can live in and above it. We may affirm what some call "mythological realism," a blending of the real with fantasy, a way of getting at truth other than by logic or scientific research. But we also insist that to ask adults to believe such stories in the Bible as history is like asking them to believe in childish fairy tales.

So if we bother with the early Bible stories, we don't go to them as we might to a telephone book, looking for factual data. We try to read between the lines, searching for symbolic meaning in the characters' experience and behavior, as when we watch myth-based film series such as *Lord of the Rings, Star Wars,* and *Star Trek.* We contend that to see the hero of the Rings series, Frodo, as legendary and nonhistorical does not invalidate the truths the storyteller Tolkien wants us to face. In the same way, when we say that Adam and Eve were mythological figures it does not undermine what the biblical storytellers wanted their people to understand about their humanity.

So, no, we don't believe that a few thousand years ago a snake actually stood on its tail or hung from a branch and spat out Hebrew verb forms at two human beings named Adam and Eve. We think that story is silly as history; it trivializes any meaning it has and turns people off who are informed, intelligent, and do their own responsible thinking. Some Spiritual Secularists may explore what the story says about us and what it calls us to do and be. For example, we might say that, like Adam and Eve, we often are our own worst enemies. We behave in ways that undercut our best interests and then blame our parents, siblings, coworkers, or the Devil—anyone but ourselves. One thing the story tells us is that such behavior is our downfall.

Those who believe the Bible to be God's eternal Word, and who take it all literally, are shocked by our way of interpreting it. They don't think it is their business to interpret the Bible, but to *believe it*. They don't think they are *interpreting* scripture when they take its stories literally. In addition, they say that the Bible itself says God directly inspired it all, and they charge us Spiritual Secularists with not believing the Bible. In one sense, we must plead guilty; and we're happy to do so. Again, we may be convinced the Bible has some important things to say, but we refuse to idolize it. As people with some open association with Christianity, we are embarrassed by the dreadful literalism and absolute certainty that *true believers* possess about their interpretations. We also deplore the serious nonsense and insidious mischief caused by their idolatry.

It Claims Sole Possession of Truth

This Church teaching goes hand-in-glove with idolatry of the Bible. We Spiritual Secularists believe it violates the heart and thrust of Jesus' gospel. Fundamentalists and evangelicals insist that Christianity holds the only true way to God. While there are other scriptures, for our purpose here, it's sufficient to return to the verse Rick Warren quoted to Charlie Rose. Jesus tells his disciples: "I am the way, the truth and the life; no one comes to the Father but by me." (John 14:6). Based on this passage alone, traditional Christianity has been comfortable teaching that those who won't or don't believe in Jesus, and those who never heard of him, will spend eternity separated from God.

How do we Spiritual Secularists handle this passage? We take it to mean *the exact opposite* of what fundamentalists and evangelicals say it means.

Stop and think for a moment about what Jesus calls his *way*. The Gospels consistently portray him as being "narrow-minded about being broadminded"; or, to use another paradox, "intolerant of intolerance." Let those sink in for a moment.

Now note that the same Gospel writer quotes Jesus as earlier telling his disciples: "Other sheep have I that are not of this fold" (John 10:16). The disciples didn't like Jesus affirming those who were outside their flock. When people in a Samaritan town were nasty to their teacher (Luke 9:54), two of his disciples wanted him to "call down fire from heaven" that would consume them. Jesus soundly rebuked them. He defined his *way* by embracing not only lepers, the poor, disreputable women, and other social outcasts, but also, you may remember, the hated Samaritans we talked of earlier. The traditional, unthinking, *exclusive* interpretation of John 14:6 is totally out of step with Jesus' way of being *exclusively inclusive*.

With regard to Jesus' second phrase, "I am the truth," it is precisely his openness to, or respect for, everyone, that embodies what it means to be a *living truth*—that is, to be an authentic human being who is true to herself or himself. And being an authentic person is *the life!*

This coin has two sides. On one side, I hear Jesus say that people who will not be open-minded and practice *exclusive inclusiveness* cannot know what it is to be complete, or whole, or authentic. And that's a dreadful sadness. But on the other side, I read him to say that anyone who will love lavishly can "come to his Father," because his God is all-inclusive love. I John 4:16 says: "God is love" (the Greek word is *agape*, the inclusive love I've been talking about), "and the one who dwells in *agape* dwells in God, and God in him." When we know of this acceptance, no matter how our knowledge came to us, and we accept it, it frees us in turn to practice inclusive *agape*, that is, to accept and respect even those whom we dislike or who consider themselves our enemies. This *gospel* says we all are accepted no matter what we believe or how we behave. At the same time, it warns us of the negative personal consequences of not behaving out of love.

We Spiritual Secularists assume that no one religion possesses the only way to ultimate truth, or Nirvana, or wholeness, or contact with whatever we mean by the name God. We also don't believe that all religions, or worldviews, or philosophies—especially narrow-minded, intolerant or exclusive ones—enrich us deeply and generate personal wholeness. At the same time, we value all worldviews—philosophical or spiritual, Western or Eastern, religious or secular—that are open-minded, tolerant and *exclusively inclusive.*

In summary, here are the two basic ways those associated with Christianity see the significance of Jesus:

> **Traditional and Supernatural.** Sin separates us from God in heaven. God loved us so much he sent his son Jesus to earth to pay for our sin and make us acceptable to Him. If you will turn from your sin and toward God's love, and trust Jesus to be your Savior, you will be forgiven and go to heaven when you die. (*Turn* and you won't *burn.*) Those who haven't heard of Jesus, or don't trust Him, are unforgiven and out of luck. And that's their problem, so they can go to hell.
>
> **Spiritual and Secular:** The *agapaic* love that determined Jesus' values accepts everyone, including those who don't turn to Jesus and those who have never heard of him. It transforms for wholeness all those who embrace the idea that to respect oneself and everyone else—that is, to be *exclusively inclusive*—is *the way, the truth and the life.* But those who don't hear that they are loved, or who hear it but simply don't get it, or can't accept it, will not enjoy their acceptance or be enriched by accepting everyone else.

As a Spiritual Secularist who at one time proclaimed the supernatural view of Jesus as Savior, I have come to see it as a distortion of his gospel. I now view the Spiritual Secularist view as the genuine good news— even if it includes, and perhaps because it includes, an apt warning about the dehumanizing effects of narrow-mindedness.

In the end, Spiritual Secularists see all peacemaking religions and philosophies as trying to address the same central mysteries. We look on their devotees as fellow "cosmic vagabonds" in the quest for a world of fair play and a lasting peace. We don't hold that all their beliefs are true and helpful—some are plainly false and destructive. But we are convinced the world desperately needs all people of faith, and of *unfaith*, to work hand-in-hand toward a sustainable future. So, rather than being dragged kicking and screaming to cooperate with people of other faiths, we Spiritual Secularists, if anything, support and even initiate such efforts. And no, we don't always find the road open or easy going.

It Plays the Heaven and Hell Card

Many ancient cultures held to mythologies that had good and bad places to which people go when they die. Life has always been mysterious, difficult, and painful for many people, and it can be a source of great comfort to them to believe that when you die you go to a beautiful place of bliss and get to stay there forever.

Judaism never has had a serious doctrine of the afterlife. The God of Abraham was concerned with the secular life and practices of His people. Priests represented the people to God. Their role was to shape the religious life of Israel. They helped the people keep their holy days and perform their sacrifices to appease God's wrath and attain His blessings on their nation and their individual lives. They didn't talk about heaven and hell.

While the priests spoke to God about the people, the prophets spoke to the people on behalf of God. These real heroes of ancient Israel quoted God in condemning the nation for its tolerance of iniquity and crookedness, its indifference to social and economic injustice and its lack of compassion for the weak and poor. They also report that what particularly infuriates God is that, at the same time, they are going through the mechanical motions of religious life. But here again, God's concern is not that they so live that they can go to heaven when they die, but that they will live with such character that they will experience a heavenly quality of life on Earth. Still today religious and nonreligious Jews alike look for a heaven on earth. You can get a fast feel for God's secular orientation by reading the very short, biblical book of Amos.

Biblical scholars agree that Jesus' Sermon on the Mount (Matthew 5-7) that I referred to back in Chapter 9, was not one sermon but a collection of some of the central points Jesus sought to make to his followers. He makes no reference to heaven and hell. In the early days of Christianity that I also reviewed earlier, we saw the Church's main message change from creating loving community on Earth to promising eternal bliss in heaven. The message went from *transformation* of our world in this life to *transportation* to a better world in the next one.

Despite what we now know today about human nature and the staggering expanse of the cosmos, combined with our knowledge of ancient mythologies and superstition, traditional churches continue to say that if you believe in God as they do, or keep the Ten Commandments, or observe the sacraments, or contribute your money and time to the church, or trust in Jesus as your savior—depending on the church to which you are listening—you will go up to heaven when you die instead of down to the horrors of hell. Yes, most churches tell you to keep the Golden Rule *here and now*. But their dominant concern is to make sure you do not go in the *hereafter* to the Devil, along with ignorant, bad, and unbelieving people.

Traditional churches make the afterlife central to their message. They have adopted the role of the Great Comforter. They see themselves as God's appointed "fire insurance" agencies. This fits with their taking ancient mythology literally and hyping a supernatural, exclusive view of salvation. It seems quite clear to objective observers that churches use the threat of eternal punishment and the lure of everlasting delight to keep people in their folds and secure obedience to their dictates.

Because we live in a culture that hears a good bit about heaven and hell, we have tended, perhaps unconsciously, to assume that these places are real. For those not reared in the Church, it may be easy to *imagine,* as John Lennon suggests, that there's no heaven or hell. But for those programmed to believe in an afterlife, giving up the hope of heaven can be threatening and painful, especially if family and friends count on you to support their belief. Whether it was easy or difficult, we Spiritual Secularists are among those who have put the heaven and hell myths to rest. We don't obsess on the afterlife. We don't accept the notion that a loving God has set things up so that the overwhelming majority of His offspring in a future life will forever suffer excruciating torture due to their ignorance, failures, misdeeds, and unbelief in this life. We join the atheists, agnostics, pagans, and other *bad* people in believing that the idea of our continuing in some good form of who we are after we die is wishful thinking.

As Spiritual Secularists who connect to Christianity, we reject the afterlife fixation for several reasons. For one, we have learned that the universe isn't made up of heaven above and hell below and that talking about going in either direction, whether from Chicago or China, makes no sense whatsoever. We understand the desire to transcend death and find "peace at the last," but we find no evidence of a supernatural reality out there, a realm of reality separate from our own universe.

We also note that traditional Christians who tout heaven and hell invariably distort two biblical concepts associated with Jesus' gospel. The first is eternal life. According to the main corps of biblical scholars, the New Testament, when seen through the lens of a Hebrew worldview, says that eternal life is not an endless string of days we go through after we die. It's not a category of *quantity*—it pertains to a spiritually transformed *quality* of life right now.

The second mishandled term is *the Kingdom of Heaven*. In the Gospels, it's used interchangeably with *the Kingdom of God,* and depicts, not a place to which you go when you die, but the enriching, fulfilled social reality controlled by the freedom, justice, and peace that Israel's prophets said their God wanted for them. In other words, *kingdom* has to do with a type of *reign*, not a *realm;* it's concerned with spiritual *governance*, not *geography*.

A clarification of these two central notions of Christian faith raises grave questions about the Church's preoccupation with an afterlife of heaven and hell. It also helps explain why, contrary to the other-worldly way the traditional Church understands Jesus' gospel, we see it as this-worldly, or secular. We view Jesus as one who had his feet on the ground and showed us how to apply the spirit of *agape* to family, social, political, and economic realities. His worldview shapes how we think and speak about public issues.

We see Jesus' secular significance in his assuming not the mantle of the temple-bound religious priest but those of the roving, nonreligious prophet, the wisdom teacher and the healer. In him, we see *agape* working at the cultural flashpoints that make and break human lives. In the same way today, this love seeks to transform life not so much in sanctuaries one day a week, but every day in factories and offices where people work, in the malls where they spend their money, and in laboratories and universities that are fountains of creativity and new knowledge.

We Spiritual Secularists relish the sense of self-worth and positive energy we experience from trusting that we are accepted and loved just as we are. We note that *agape* effects a dynamic breakthrough from the sterile obligation not to do what is wrong--the debt imposed by law--to a robust, liberating, spiritual power to do what is right. We believe that such love is precisely the solid foundation we all need for an ethically sensitive spirituality in the midst of the human predicament. We find ourselves enriched, even as we commit to do what we can to keep human life human by making this a better world for all who inhabit it. And we are convinced that the *agape* so pregnant in Jesus will nourish and dignify everyone open to its power.

In the realm of personal ethics, Jesus insists that his followers forsake revenge and respect their enemies. He wants them to resist evil but put an end to violence as a form of self-defense and political strategy. We hear him call for compassion toward the most vulnerable among us; and for changes in our social structures so that the needy don't fall between the cracks. We interpret his call as asking his people to reject the callous governance and economics created by dictators, senates or, apropos of today, greedy, super-profitable corporations. We also affirm his obvious concern that the men in charge provide places of welcome and equality for women, homosexuals, ethnic minorities, the handicapped, and for any others who've been browbeaten by the social order. Sadly, we don't find these secular/spiritual matters on the agenda of many churches.

Even Spiritual Secularists who are not associated with Christianity gain inspiration and ethical direction from Jesus' commitment to create a compassionate world of peace and justice. They see his preoccupation with transforming *this world,* as spiritually appealing. They also find him bigger than rationality. He taps into mystery and is outrageous with paradox. ("Lose your life to find it.") He's demanding as well as compelling, because, as someone has said: "His career has the quality of a showdown." He refuses to settle for the *status quo;* he relentlessly pushes the moral order's envelope and tells us never to let our primal, animalistic needs, alone, dictate how we relate to ourselves and to others.

With such understanding, Spiritual Secularists associated in some way with Jesus are humble enough to allow that, while a vast majority of Americans claims to be Christian, there really are very few anywhere worthy of the name.

It Perpetuates Animal Sacrifice Atonement

Still another hallmark of traditional Christianity that alienates Spiritual Secularists is what the Church makes of the cross. As noted earlier, both Roman Catholicism and fundamentalist and Evangelical Protestants continue to view Jesus' death as a human sacrifice, modeled after, or in fulfillment of, the sacrifices of animals offered ritualistically by priests in ancient Hebrew temples.

The mythologies and religious texts of many prehistoric cultures worldwide show that they made not only animal, but human, sacrifices to gain the favor of their gods. They tended to kill virgins untainted by sex, first-born males, and members of their tribes considered to be evil or weak.

In the earliest days of ancient Israel, prominent figures thought they were told by God to practice human sacrifice (Google "human sacrifice in the Bible"). Do you remember the story of Abraham and his son Isaac? He reportedly hears God tell him that to prove he's afraid of God he is to slay his son and then set his body on fire as a burnt offering sacrifice (Genesis 22:1-18). Over and over during this biblical age we are told that the Hebrews' God loves the smell of burning flesh. Abraham goes to the appointed place, builds an altar and has Isaac lie upon it. Just as he holds a dagger to his son's throat to slit it, however, he hears the voice of an angel tell him not to do it, for he has *proven that he fears God.* When he looks around, caught in a nearby thicket is a ram, which he slays—instead of Isaac—as a sacrifice to please his God.

Whether this is an historical account or one of those stories told to make some kind of point, each of us can decide. History or myth, however, surely the idea, that a father should kill his son to please voices he hears from the sky is sick or evil. And if his religion holds that what he heard truly was God's voice and will, the same judgments hold true for it. If today we hear that a father has had the thought of killing his son, we send him to a shrink. If a father kills his child to please God we charge him with the heinous crime of murder, put him in jail and throw away the key. Some believe this story may have been told to stop Israel from practicing human sacrifice, to tell them God wants them to know there is *a better way*, even if it is animal sacrifice. If so, we might view it, then, as a sign of the work of *agape* in cultural evolution. We also can be grateful that early in the onset of historical record-keeping, this nation, along with most other cultures, saw the barbarism in human sacrifice and ceased the practice.

As I noted before, the earliest Christians tell us that the Hebrew God loves the world so much that He masterminds the sacrifice of His own Son, Jesus, to atone for the sins of all humankind, and that he arranges for his bloody death to be carried out by the evil oppressors of his people. In the shadow of animal sacrifices, Jesus' followers come to see him as the sacrificial *Lamb of God* destined to save the world from its sin. He has to die a bloody death, for "without the shedding of blood there is no forgiveness" (Hebrews 9:22). In this transaction, their God satisfies his own wrathful judgment against sin, and those who trust Jesus as their Savior, they say, get a free pass to everlasting heavenly bliss. I've already mentioned what happens to all those who lived and died before Jesus came along, those for whom this transaction doesn't make any sense, and those who never have heard of Jesus.

Around 70 AD, as also noted earlier, when the temple in Jerusalem was destroyed, the Pharisees got Judaism to stop killing animals on their temple altars. But because the early Christians were Jewish and used to the dramatic ritual of animal sacrifice, we find its imagery in the New Testament, and much of the Church continues to perpetuate the symbolism. In the same way in our time, along with most progressive Christians, Spiritual

Secularists have dropped the *blood-payment* theory about the crucifixion and taken one step further away from a barbaric God.

For us, Jesus voluntarily made himself vulnerable in both his life and death as a *spiritual* sacrifice for his oppressed people and for all who suffer everywhere. The cross stands for the depth, breadth and length of *agape*, that total, or perfect expression of love. Thus it stands as the crowning witness to his commitment to heal the world and to summon all who would participate in that healing with him. ("Take up your cross and follow me." Mark 8:34)

When we look at Jesus' early death from a contemporary human standpoint, we might say that he was in fact done in by his own preposterous message about loving your enemies, resisting them nonviolently, and not using the sword to defend yourself, fight other tribes or build empires. His radical message of *agape* so exposed and condemned Rome for its cruelty that its provincial ruler in Jerusalem, Pilate, couldn't stand it and had him killed for it. One could say, therefore, that Jesus died not *for* the world's sins but *because of* them.

What is truly significant about Jesus' sacrificial death is his unlimited compassion and concern for justice, peace and freedom—it was his love of these critical, virtuous human values that led to his inevitable, violent end. It was, of course, the *agape* that drove Jesus that also directed the lives and led to the tragic deaths of such modern heroes as Gandhi and Martin Luther King, Jr. So, we view the cross as a call to the love of which there is none greater, and a sign of hope for this world. But we also see it as a warning of what it can cost to care so much for your fellow human beings that you speak the truth to those who hold power unjustly, whether religious or political. (Is it no wonder there never have been very many genuine Christians?)

We note, too, that Jesus' willingness to die for a redemptive cause shows us that faith is not simply a matter of uncritical belief in the Bible, or in Church-designed dogma, or in anyone's writings, including mine. Faith begins with trusting that it is *agape* that brings healing warmth and spiritual light to this world. Then, it is so living that you become another source of that warmth and light.

This way of looking at Jesus' death may not impress Evangelicals. But as a Spiritual Secularist, I find it biblical, reasonable, humbling, and compelling.

It Distorts the Born-Again Experience

This marvelous phrase speaks of starting life over, an experience we all might relish. About 2000 years ago, the Gospel writer John reported on a brief conversation Jesus had had with a man to whom he said, "You must be born again." Christian evangelists, using television in the last half of the twentieth century, inserted the term *born again* into the American secular vocabulary. Whether or not you are one of the 50 million Americans who claim to be "born again," you have heard the phrase.

Feelings of guilt, unworthiness, and even worthlessness have driven many to accept Jesus as their Savior in hopes of starting a brand-new life. Evangelist Billy Graham's tactic in a typical two-week crusade was to spend the first week preaching about sin and hell to make listeners feel terrible about themselves and afraid of God's judgment (it's referred to as "being under the conviction of sin"). The next week he cranked up the love-of-Jesus message to get people jumping out of their seats and coming forward to be saved, or "born again." The emotional impact was often stunning, often life-changing.

Christian fundamentalists and evangelicals use the phrase to identify their exhilarating inner-life, new consciousness when they accepted Jesus as their Savior. They received the message that he had died for their sins and that they would be accepted by God despite what they were like and what they had done, if they would only trust him to save them; and when they did it was as if Christ took residence in their hearts. With this new life, they felt as if they'd been catapulted into heaven. Indeed, the kicker for the newly born-again person is that both the Bible-quoting evangelist and the new sense of where you stand with God tell you that heaven is where you are going when you die. In born-again circles, the new birth of someone who's a celebrity from the world of sport, entertainment, or politics, or who's lived a particularly sinful life (the worse the better), is paraded as evidence that the second birth can save us from ourselves, the human predicament and hell itself. No wonder the phrase "born again" packs a wallop.

As one who has been born again, let me tell you my story.

When I was twelve, my parents sent me to Shadowbrook, a summer camp in the Pocono Mountains of Pennsylvania run by the evangelist Percy Crawford. They hoped that in one week, Crawford, who preached daily to the campers, would "scare the hell out of me," and I would be "saved." Their plan worked. The man was a master manipulator of young, undeveloped minds and of raw emotions. (Of course, I didn't see this at the time; remember, I was twelve.)

Despite, and perhaps because of, Crawford's blatantly manipulative tactics, his overt passion and his simplistic, other-worldly, God-loves-you view of the Christian gospel, as he spoke something about the glory of *agape* got through to me. A light bulb went on in my head! (*Aha!*). After one more of Crawford's talks, a camp counselor, following up in a private conversation pressed this point: "Because God is love, Jesus died to save us all from our sin. If I will accept him as my Savior, then God will accept me, and I will go to heaven to be with God when I die." I chose to trust Jesus. And I was born again.

If before this experience someone had asked whether I knew Jesus loved me, I no doubt would have said, "Yes, Jesus loves me." For years I had this drummed into me through a little ditty we sang in Sunday school: "Jesus loves me, this I know, for the Bible tells me so." But now, at just twelve, I had both mental and experiential frameworks for thinking about the significance of such love for all of life. My experience recast how I thought and felt about God, other people, and myself—I now saw myself as one who was defined by *agape*. I don't mean that I fully understood *agape* or respectfully loved everyone. I didn't; and I still don't. But for the first time I came to appreciate what I knew of it as the key to being real and finding both a critical sense of connection and joy. And since then, *agape* has made me want to go out of my way to treat everyone with compassion and respect, even some people I can't stand.

My point here is that I don't see everything about the "born again" experience as bad, or as a problem.

But there *are* problems.

Perhaps the best way to get into them is to first ask this question: What could Spiritual Secularists possibly have against the idea of being born again? Examine that with me in the next few pages.

First, we must acknowledge that not everyone who is part of a church, or who professes to be a Christian, claims to have had the born-again experience. Some, as children, basked in the love of their parents. When told that God loved them as their parents did—that he accepted them no matter what they would do or fail to do—they transferred their parents' acceptance to God. Others who claim to be Christians came, perhaps slowly, to an understanding of *agape* at an academic or intellectual level through reading the Bible, or works of theology. Such Christians may not be able to pinpoint when, or even *whether*, they have had a born again experience. Those who promote the *second birth* tend to look on these believers with suspicion, because Jesus said: "You must be born again."

Right there is a clue as to one reason why the born-again movement disturbs Spiritual Secularists. It bluntly divides the human family between *saved* and *unsaved*. We're back to Christian exclusiveness and heaven and hell myths.

I believe many evangelists have employed the new birth metaphor sincerely. I also think they have manipulated its emotional power and both distorted and trivialized its meaning, doing their converts a great disservice. They invariably create two serious problems. First, they sell their converts on the idea that they have been totally transformed. Newly born-again people know they've been hit with a powerful change agent. In many ways, however, they remain the same; and it's not all to the good. Thus, they often feel like failures. If Christ lives in them, why do they still act like normal, sinful human beings?

In reality, of course, their old human nature remains. They have the same DNA, temperament, personality, and hormones they had as a result of their first birth. Furthermore, nothing changes regarding their sexuality. They continue to experience sexual passions and vivid, gross fantasies, and they tend to engage in the same sexual behaviors as their unsaved friends. A sad irony arises here, because fundamentalists and evangelicals put any sex outside of marriage, and unconventional sex within it, at the head of their list of horrible sins. So the newly born again soon learn that to be esteemed in their church culture they must hide their essential sexuality and humanity. As a result, they have a hard time being real to themselves and to others.

I'm sure born-again Christians want to be responsible with sex. Nevertheless, the natural urges remain and severe sexual repression and pretense invariably inflame them. Those so afflicted are told to deal with fantasies and urges through prayer and self-denial. Some former fundamentalists—at least men among them—testify openly that, during the period they were devoted to their faith, they masturbated obsessively to relieve sexual tensions. They did so, all the while pretending they would never think of doing such a thing. They also say that denial and prayer made things worse, inflicting on them inordinate psychological and emotional damage due to sexual confusion, shame and self-loathing.

If the first problem with being born again is that it doesn't change believers in the way its proponents claim, the second problem is that it tends to change people into exactly the opposite of the kind of persons Jesus had in mind. This becomes clear when we examine the encounter between Jesus and Nicodemus (Gospel of John, Chapter 3). If you are not familiar with the story, or don't have a New Testament, Google "Nicodemus" and read any number of links to it. Now allow me a little room to make my point.

It's important to note first that Nicodemus is the only person in the Four Gospels to whom Jesus said, "You must be born again." He told the woman caught in adultery that she should, "Go and sin no more." He said to the lame man, "Take up your bed and walk." He told a terrified woman to "Go in peace." He instructed the young ruler in love with his riches to sell his goods and "give the money to the poor." Jesus may have told others they needed a spiritual rebirth, but the Gospels only report his saying these words to Nicodemus.

Why was Nicodemus the one person to whom Jesus said that he needed to be born again?

We learn at least three things about the man from the first seven verses of John 3. First, he was a Pharisee, a proud leader in Judaism's "religious right." The Jews were ruled by a Roman governor, Pontius

Pilate. The Pharisees curried favor with Pilate by agreeing to keep the common people calm. In other words, Nicodemus was among those who supported the foreign military occupation--he didn't work against the oppressors in behalf of the impoverished citizenry, most of whom simply wanted food, shelter, freedom, and some justice and peace.

Because of their allegiance to Roman authority, the Pharisees kept their distance from anti-establishment troublemakers. We're not told why Nicodemus wants to see Jesus, but the writer tells us that he, understandably, steals away under the dark of night to meet Jesus for the first time. He immediately greets Jesus with a compliment: "Teacher, we know you must be from God, because nobody can do what you've done unless God is with him." Nicodemus may have been impressed with what he'd heard about Jesus, but he speaks first to impress the popular miracle worker with his own knowledge. From that we learn a second thing about Nicodemus as a religious leader—he thinks he knows it all.

Jesus offers a forthright reply that tells us he is not snowed by his know-it-all visitor. He says to Nicodemus: "Get this straight: You have to be born again. The one who is not born anew" (whose consciousness isn't transformed by a whole new way of looking at things) "cannot see the kingdom of God" (won't be able to see the possibility for God's reign in the Roman-dominated world).

Nicodemus obviously didn't get it. He asks Jesus: "How can an old man be reborn? Can he go back into his mother's womb and come out again?" Could this supposedly learned man's response have been more childish and stupid?

From these two questions we learn a third important thing about him: He interprets everything literally. He apparently can't handle metaphors, figures of speech, allegory, poetic symbolism, or matters of spirit. He needs everything in black-and-white, factual terms. His head is as hard as a rock, and Jesus' analogy that compares spiritual transformation to a second birth hasn't penetrated it.

Jesus gets right back on him: "No, no, you jackass!" (Jackass is my translation.) "You are thinking flesh, and I am talking spirit. Get it straight, numbskull: You must be changed."

Now, here's the irony and second problem with the born again movement. Evangelists and preachers tell everyone they can make feel guilty for their sins that they must be born again. All the while, they fall into Nicodemus' mindset and, irony of ironies, exhibit the same spiritual style and weaknesses we see in him:

1). They almost always are part of the religious right, supporting the *status quo* dominated by the rich and telling the vulnerable to accept injustice and poverty ("It will be better in the next life!").

2). They know it all. They claim absolute certainty regarding just about everything, because God has given them all the answers in the Bible.

3). They are not ashamed of being *literalists*, insisting that those who are born again believe everything in the Bible is factual truth.

Don't miss this irony: Those telling everyone they must be "born again" show the very same pride, arrogance, and restrictive mindset Nicodemus exhibited--and he is the very one Jesus insisted must be born again.

Because Jesus' phrase, "born again," compares spiritual birth to physical birth, we rightly see it as an experience to jump-start personal growth, the goal of which is maturity. As a result of their own distortions, however, today's evangelists indoctrinate their *spiritual babies* to keep them childish: They are to interpret the Bible literally, to love not this world but focus on the afterlife, to be simple-minded and not engage in critical thinking, and to defend God's eternal truth. Does anyone with any human knowledge at all attribute such behaviors to maturity?

The idea of maturity suggests growth toward *childlikeness* but not *childishness*; toward open-mindedness rather than narrow-mindedness; toward humility, not arrogance. Any authentic new birth will free people to take seriously the search for truth, because personal maturity only has integrity when achieved in touch with the real world. It also will compel them to pursue compassion, freedom, and justice for everyone, those spiritual and secular social values at the heart of Jesus' spirit and worldview. Sadly, these are not the marks of the new birth evangelists are peddling and producing today.

Spiritual Secularists associated in some way with Christianity reject the distortions in Christian practice today of what Jesus meant by being born again.

It Promotes Magic-Working Prayer

Spiritual Secularists associated with Christianity understand the value of taking timeout to stabilize oneself for wholeness. In the midst of a chaotic world, to schedule silence for mindful meditation, contemplation and prayer has eased symptoms of anxiety and depression for people, produced physical health benefits and helped them live balanced, worthwhile lives. We also realize there always will be mystery and surprises in nature and in human affairs, especially as they relate to the healing process and the outcomes of medical treatments. But we insist we must not affirm anything contrary to thoughtful observations about what is and what is not real.

Most devout Christians will tell you that prayer ranks at the top of spiritual exercises. They hold to myriad ideas as to what prayer is, how it is best conducted and what it will mean to you. They say it meets a deep human need because it turns you toward God. Some also see it as a duty, because God wants you to pray, and those who pray, they say, please God. Most pious practitioners tend to think of prayer in terms of confession, praise, thanksgiving, dedication, and, of course, petition--asking God for forgiveness, guidance, money, success, healing, or most anything else under the sun you desire or believe to be important.

Confessing your sins is basic to Christian prayer, for it miraculously repairs your relationship with God. If you don't do that repair work, asking God for favors becomes an empty exercise. If young people engage in lurid sexual thoughts and masturbation (which almost everyone does), they are told to confess their sins to God or a priest so they can be forgiven. I assume you and I believe that control of powerful sexual urges is important, because unbridled sex can hurt you, or other people, or your relationships with them. It may help for adults to remind the young of these dangers, but it is just as important to reassure them that, despite their infatuation with sex, they are not evil for it and are acceptable human beings. I believe it is healthy and important to confess and apologize to others when we hurt them in some way. Constant confession to God about sexual matters construed as sin strikes me as silly and probably counterproductive. Might not incessant confession of our preoccupation with sexual pleasures bore any thoughtful God and, at the same time, deepen our obsession with it? If we believe in confession, perhaps we ought to own up instead to our disregard for the victims of oppression, genocide, our culture of rape, and the glamorization of war that every day wound and kill tens of thousands of innocents, including children. I don't know of any real confession of this sort going on anywhere, especially in churches that say they hold prayer in high regard.

We Spiritual Secularists don't believe there is a Cosmic Answering Service at the other end of a prayer line. We have no problem with the thoughtful prayers of meditation I mentioned above, if they help people get their bearings for a loving, productive life. What bothers us are religious leaders who sell prayer as a magic-like power that can solve your problems. ("Have you prayed about it?")

Praying on behalf of others in need is called intercessory prayer. Here are a few examples:

> "Father in Heaven, keep watch over our soldiers at war."
> "Please, God, cure his cancer; he's such a devout believer."
> "Dear God, our boy is lost; please help us find him safe."
> "O God, my husband has lost his job. We need help."

Many serious Christians contend that if you offer such fervent intercessory prayers, God will step in to alter the natural order of things; that is, he will perform miracles to meet your needs. People actually believe this, though there is no evidence that what we mean by real miracles happens as the result of prayer. What would it take for me to believe in this kind of prayer? I'd be impressed if, all things being equal, 100 percent of cancer patients for whom loved ones prayed were cured, as opposed to the normal 40 percent. I'd also have to rethink my position if, when parents turn over to their Heavenly Father the safety of their children as the kids leave for church camp in rickety school buses, no buses ever turned over and no children ever died in them. I'd quickly change my tune, too, if, when a man's leg is amputated after an auto accident and his family, friends, and faith community pray night and day that God will give him a new leg, a new leg actually grows on his torso during the night, or over the next month, or, even, say, within his lifetime. (Scientists tell us that wounded salamanders regenerate their legs, tail, upper and lower jaw, eyes, lungs, heart, and even parts of their brain and spinal cord in a few weeks time without, as far as we know, praying about it. Has that ever happened with humans? I'm not aware of it. One might ask believers: Does God like salamanders over humans?)

Some believers may acknowledge and lamewnt the lack of evidence that God answers such prayers, but they also may value the placebo effect: If you think prayer works, they say, it will, or at least you'll feel better thinking that it does. And, if people tell you they are praying for you, your spirit will be lifted and positive energy will affect your physical healing ... even if they don't actually bother to pray. Recent studies, however, discredit this idea as it relates to those who go through major surgery. Controlled experiments showed that patients who are told they are being prayed for not only do not experience better medical results than those who aren't told this, but they also, in cases where their surgeries prove unsuccessful, become more depressed and confused because their high expectations, based on the promise of prayer, have not been fulfilled.

Traditional Christian authorities will tell you that if you pray for protection, God will take care of you. But do we have one shred of evidence for that? And is it psychologically healthy to keep asking God to give us what we want or think we need? Would a good Father in heaven (any more than an earthly father) expect and encourage his adult children to be childishly dependent, or to be self-centered and greedy? We may believe the spiritual force we call *God* supports and comforts us when we need help. But can people who are thinking at all say with any assurance that, if they pray sincerely, God will protect them from the common cold, natural disasters, accidents, fatal diseases, investment mistakes, the natural consequences of their decisions and behavior, or from death?

Nonreligious types may offer prayers to calm their frazzled nerves, lower their cholesterol, make a killing on the stock market, or to hit a home run. But even the most pious believers acknowledge that some petitions are superficial, foolish and egotistical. Especially worthy of ridicule are those that ask God to save them from the consequences of irresponsible behavior.

"Dear Jesus! Help me pass this test. Next time I'll study."
"Yikes! I'm doing 85! Oh, God, don't let me get a ticket!"
"Ooooh God! Dear God! Don't let me get pregnant!"

A few years back a CNN journalist reportedly went to Jerusalem in search of a story. She had heard of a devout old man well known for having gone every day of his adult life to pray at the Western Wall, and received permission to check him out. She flew to Tel Aviv, hired a limo for the drive to Jerusalem, and went directly to the wall. She asked those who might know the man where she could find him, and one pointed him out to her as he stood against the wall nodding his head in prayer. After twenty minutes or so, as he prepared to leave, she approached him, identified herself with CNN, and asked for an interview. He was perplexed, but nodded yes, and she began.

She: *How long have you been coming to the Wall to pray?*
He: *For more than half a century.*
She: *And what do you pray for?*
He: *For peace between the Jews and Arabs. For all the hatred to stop. For our children to grow up in safety and friendship.*
She: *And how do you feel after doing this for over 50 years?*
He: *Like I'm talking to a fucking wall.*

Most religious leaders don't inform their followers that prayers will sometimes go unanswered and that there will be lonely times in which

God will seem absent. When prayers do go unanswered, they often tell believers that God obviously answered them with a *No*, or that what they were praying for must not be good for them or is not part of God's plan. For their part, atheists say that God doesn't answer prayers and seems absent because God never has been present. Spiritual Secularists say that, if you are trying to manipulate the "Magic-working Man Upstairs," and he doesn't answer, and he seems absent, inept or even cruel, it's because the magic-working God isn't real.

Spiritual Secularists remain unimpressed with those who claim that miracles happen with prayer, who make rigid rules about prayer, who press us to pray a lot, who want us to say grace in a crowded restaurant, or who rate us spiritually by our devotion to what they think prayer is. I find that such judgments about prayer hinder us from becoming full and free adults.

It Offers Little Grace and Truth

We've just covered six traditional Christian church teachings that Spiritual Secularists associated with Christianity find offensive for their lack of self-awareness, integrity and grace: 1) worshiping the Bible; 2) claiming exclusive possession of the truth; 3) using Heaven and Hell to manipulate people; 4) perpetuating the animal sacrifice theory of how you get right with God; 5) distorting the born-again experience; and 6) promoting magic-making prayer. We now look at how traditional churches operate and why they turn us off.

Earlier we noted that the Gospels tell us that Jesus formed a ragtag group of disciples he dubbed his *called-out ones,* or his *Church.* We looked at some of the radically different forms Church has taken over its long history. We reviewed the early persecuted, fractured Church that suffered for a couple of centuries under Rome, the longtime, domineering Roman Catholic Church of Medieval times, the emergence of Protestantism and the European state churches over the past five centuries, and the wild mix of Catholic, Protestant, and independent churches and sects in the United States today.

Many church persons who were indoctrinated when young end up stuck in parishes that fit their upbringing. Other emotionally or psychologically dependent types are drawn to churches that major in the security of conformity, and they remain there. But the majority of educated, assertive adults between college age and fifty stand outside any form of church. One could say that that is how it always has been. Over our history, most Americans in their productive years have focused on making money, or establishing careers, or marrying and having children, and have tended not to take much time for serious reflection. But it also is true that many adults in this age range are simply lost in our materialistic, fast-paced, digitally wound-up, and isolating world. We find it sad that many in this age range also lack either or both warmth and light in their lives, and the organized people of Jesus don't seem to speak their language or give them nonverbal signals of hospitality and hope.

Many self-invalidating incongruities of church life discourage Spiritual Secularists and others who are looking for authentic community. For one, a good number of church leaders say the Church's task is to "build the Kingdom of God on earth," or to "win the world for Christ." It's the same spirit that propelled the early Christians and spurred the missionary movements of modern times. Since the Church takes institutional form, it also is captive in this country to the business model that calls for "grow, grow, grow" and says "bigger is better." It's the commission that has caused churches and Christians to be self-righteously condescending, proud and pushy in trying to convert others to their beliefs. Somehow, it also is tied into the clergy's assumption that, to please God, satisfy their egos and be seen as successful, they must work hard to earn promotions to bigger and bigger churches. By contrast, more thoughtful Christians have cast their purpose in terms not of *winning* others to Christ, but simply of trying to *bear witness* by word and deed to the *agapaic* love that Jesus demonstrated. They don't presume to be building the Kingdom of God but to exhibit what community looks like that is shaped by compassion, healthy administration, justice and peacemaking. Spiritual Secularists find acceptable this *witness* style. The obsession with *winning*, or *being successful*, troubles them.

Also, the culture of most churches remains dated, stilted, and discordant. The language of hymns and gospel choruses is filled with repetitive references to the male Sky God. The clergy may draft prayers that attempt to be poetic, but most of them use archaic language, as if God were still living in biblical times, the Dark Ages, or at least as far back as the eighteenth century. The problem is not that nothing from the past is true or helpful; it's that since biblical times our knowledge has changed radically toward reality and for the better, and the traditional church doesn't seem to get it. Attempts to modernize by using PowerPoint presentations and the hip jargon of the day, but with the same petrified traditions and outdated thought forms (God is still "up there," and so on), often make things worse. Rituals and traditions that make sense and are in touch with what is real outside sanctuary walls can strengthen the spirit of churches, but the rituals of the typical traditional church ring of superstition and irrational sentimentality.

With its portrait of Jesus, the Gospel of John addresses not the Jews or the Romans or the Greeks but the early Church. The writer tells them that their leader's unique glory was that he was "full of grace and truth" (John 1:14). The radical forgiveness and acceptance of grace speaks of the deepest spiritual warmth. In some American churches today we discover traces of grace. But where are those that provide a radical, welcoming hospitality for all people? Where are the churches wherein grace is shockingly robust? Sadly, far too many traditional churches tend to operate by narrow conformity and promote the emotional and psychological dependency I mentioned earlier, rather than adult interdependence wherein adult-to-adult relationships set love free to flourish.

Equally important, where can we find lavish grace combined with the light of theological honesty and truth? Instead of priests and pastors encouraging people to think for themselves and take responsibility for their lives, most priests and pastors still operate parent-to-child—the *answer-man* (or woman) talks down to the theologically uninformed parishioners. How many pastors and priests challenge their members to think critically and embrace only a worldview that is internally consistent and fits the facts as we know them today?

Some churches present themselves simply as shelters from life's storms, or as infirmaries for the wounded—which, of course, all of us are, at least on occasion. Others offer "fast-food blessings" to those who will do as they are told and not ask questions. Many church plants operate, as someone has said, "like caffeinated start-up businesses driven by the fear of not growing fast enough." Still others operate as spiritual police stations—that is, sterile places of law enforcement, with climates of judgment, condemnation and rejection. And yes, some simply exist to serve as "fire escapes" to heaven. But in light of Jesus' style, should any of his followers in this enlightened age assume these patronizing roles?

Spiritual Secularists are looking for the clear ring of both grace and truth. The kinds of communities that appeal to them emphasize responsible process over rules. They set up systems and procedures that reflect what we have learned from the social and psychological sciences. They refuse to play the church game, to go through the motions of being community or to see themselves as organizations rather than living organisms. Their leaders listen to members' concerns, encourage them to ask honest questions, and challenge them to integrate their own *secularity* and spirituality. The members agree to boundaries of mutual respect, so no one's neurosis gets to run wild. If one of them violates those boundaries, the members gently but firmly call her or him to account. Sadly, institutionalism almost always strangles churches, and few seem able to organize in ways that promote such emotional, mental and spiritual health.

Traditional churches continue to be plagued by basic failures of integrity. All of them say they welcome everyone, but hardly any do—they too easily become cliques rather than communities wherein differences are welcome. They all say they care for truth, but most of them close themselves off from any new knowledge that challenges their beliefs. And even as most say they want to address current needs, they continue to live with mindsets from the distant past. Some churches transcend such flagrant self-contradictions, but they are few and far between.

What may surprise you is that many active clergy are Spiritual Secularists. The vast majority of them are closeted in the churches they serve for fear of upsetting parishioners and possibly losing their ministries, to which they may be deeply committed and upon which, of course, they depend for their livelihoods. Some pastors, who felt they had to be honest and leave the Church, lost their defined ministries. And too many who continue to minister have lost the ability to be *full of truth*. It's another sad side-effect of institutionalism.

Because we Spiritual Secularists have trouble finding what strike us as authentic churches, many of us have little or no involvement in a local congregation or parish. We continue, however, to look for congregations, parishes, house churches, spontaneous groups, para-church organizations, or other informal associations that work at being celebratory, hospitable, inclusive, reconciling, and psychologically, emotionally and intellectually healthy--providers of genuine *warmth* and *light*.

The leaders of such rare, authentic communities not only offer personal support, but they call members to carry on *a lover's quarrel* with the world. Many of the members see themselves in community to get their bearings for effective *quarreling*. They refuse to settle comfortably into social contexts rigged to support the privileged. They try to do what they can with their time, money and energy to promote, fair play and peace. At opportune times, they lock arms with organizations that do nonviolent battle with governments, corporations and other powers that by deception, greed and manipulation soil the social fabric. Very few traditional churches engage in such endeavors.

Spiritual Secularists realize we don't live in an ideal world with perfect churches. We know that were we ever to think we had found one, it would lose its perfection the moment we became members. We have chuckled with the late theologian Robert McAfee Brown, who was noted for saying, "The Church is like Noah's ark ... if it weren't for the storm outside, you couldn't stand the stink inside." But Brown did not propose running from either the world or the Church. He looked for authentic communities that cared about and celebrated justice, moral courage and mutuality. He understood that humans who battle injustice and wage peace sooner or later will find it wearying and need support. He also wanted church people to be able to think, to challenge their own beliefs and those of their churches. Are we asking too much of churches to expect that they will reflect the "grace and truth" that the Gospel writer said was so evident in Jesus?

In the American 1960s, Spiritual Secularists of all stripes stood with those at the front of the civil rights revolution, the movement to liberate women, and protests against the Vietnam War. They continue to act on the same principles in today's world. You'll find them trying to help protect the environment, combat racism, care for neglected children, free political prisoners, abolish hunger and feed the hungry, curb the AIDS epidemic, expose reactionary forces that play on people's fears and ignorance, protest imperialism and unjust wars, and engage in a myriad of other humane efforts our world so desperately needs. No, none of them covers all of these concerns, but in their times and places, they all try to embody secular and spiritual values that contribute to the common good. And most of them, ever hopeful, continue to look for authentic community ... even in churches and synagogues.

You've now looked at four major worldviews, or belief systems: 1) traditional Western religions, mainly the dominant Christianity, 2) Eastern philosophy, 3) secular science, and 4) Secular Spirituality—including its adherents with some connection to Christianity. I made my case for this last worldview, because I am convinced it both offers the warmth and light we need and avoids the narrow-mindedness of traditional religion and science.

I encourage you to keep this in mind: No matter which worldview you choose—or you create for yourself—you never can test fully or be entirely comfortable with all the data and theories you hold to be true. Human life is too complex and mysterious for that. It simply is what it is. This doesn't excuse you, however, from sorting things out and choosing insights that solidify, stabilize and give your worldview integrity. It also won't let you off the hook for living fully as a secular and spiritual member of the human family. And it does not mean you need not take that road that leads to wholeness.

So, to make your way through the predicament and spiritual swamp in front of us today, to what voices will you listen? And how will you know which path to follow?

Gaining enlightenment is like the moon reflected in the water. The moon does not get wet, nor is the water disturbed. Although its light is intensive and great, the whole moon and the whole sky are reflected in one drop of water, in a dew-drop on the grass. The depth of the drop is the height of the moon.

Zen Master Eihel Dogen

No one knows what path you should follow except yourself. You are your own wise teacher. You are your own Guru.

Grace G Payge

The intuitive mind is a sacred gift, and the rational mind is a faithful servant. We have created a society that honors the servant and has forgotten the gift.

Albert Einstein

There is no justice in the laws of nature, no term for fairness in the equations of motion. The Universe is neither evil, nor good, it simply does not care. The stars don't care, or the Sun, or the sky. But they don't have to! We care! There IS light in the world, and it is US!

Eliezer Yudkowsky

CHAPTER 13:

TESTING FOR TRUTH

Check the Voices You Hear

I've been clear that when I say *spirit*, I refer to the positive mental, emotional, moral and practical dimensions essentially unique to human consciousness. I identify them by their relation to the ordinary choices we make and the profound mysteries we encounter every day at the center of our lives. I don't pretend to have a firm grip on these mysteries. I'm fascinated by what the Zen Master says on the previous page, but I'm not sure I totally grasp its import. I suspect science can explain the reflection in the dewdrop he talks about. And I think he's not being spooky but is viewing the universe through a nonrational, nonscientific, poetic lens, which I believe is our task, too.

If our new atheists and other hard-line philosophical materialists are still sailing with us, here's where they may jump ship. The ability to measure things precisely, as the scientific method requires, does not fully apply here. So they will charge us with slipping into a realm of unreality that renders the quest for truth meaningless. I believe they're wrong and invite you to enter with me into this admittedly cloudy area in search of further depth and breadth for our lives. We'll try to discern better how we can balance the secular and spiritual to enrich our lives, and to make the world a better, life-affirming place.

As I noted earlier, we must embark on such a voyage because, for most of us, pure rationalism, materialism, and the scientific method cannot slake our inner thirst. They cannot help us find the purposes for which you and I are here, or even explain why we wonder about and seek them. They also have no reason to offer an ethic that includes self-sacrifice and respect for one's enemy, the highest, noblest of commitments. They have little scientific to say that will help us build character, relate us constructively to everyone else, and guide us toward wholeness. When we are seeking truths upon which wholeness is built, a purely secular mindset and rationalism take us only so far.

Be clear that the quest to find spiritual truth does not require that we leave reason behind. It does insist, however, that we look beyond sensory experience and analytical thinking as our only sources of knowledge. We must also seek knowledge in imagination, feeling, intuition, insight, time-tested wisdom, and commitment—even as we acknowledge that each of these sources can lead us astray. We also should know that when we jump into the murky and often swirling waters of the spiritual, our feet may not always touch bottom, and it may be terrifyingly hard to keep our heads above water and not drown. To be complete persons, however, jump we must. And even as we plunge into the tricky currents and cloudy depths we may face, we're aware that while support may be close by, it is up to us to draw on it and stay afloat, even if we don't swim.

Start at the shallow end, making sure you first get your feet wet without going in over your head. Spiritual gurus tell us that whenever we feel "in pieces," burned-out, confused, uncertain and afraid, we can find repair and fulfillment by "following our bliss" and listening to "our inner voices." But because we all hear so many voices, both from deep within us and from all around us, we must ask: "How can we know that a voice is speaking a truth that we need?" And, of course, we can't, unless we apply the two basic tests I identified earlier: internal consistency and external correspondence. In other words, we can trust a voice that 1) isn't always contradicting itself, and 2) says things that fit what we already know to be critically important and real, or true.

We must, however, apply another test. I take us back to *agape*. This spiritual power obliges us to obey voices that call us to accept and become one with others, with ourselves, and with all of creation. It insists that we shun those that tell us we can violate the rights of others or support powers that oppress the human spirit. Because it arises from the ground of our existence, this love orders us not to overindulge any bloated self-interest we may have, or to run away from the real world.

Keep in mind that when I say *agape*, I'm not talking about some *secret* of the universe in some hidden spirit world that only a few can reach. I am convinced that this love is our primary source of positive spirituality. We grasp how central it is to our lives from the profound loneliness, inner disconnect and sense of desperation we suffer if we think we're not loved and we're afraid we never may be. We also know of this love from tapping those sages whose voices resonate deep inside of us, who inspire, challenge, and bring out the best in us. We learn from great literature, too, that only when we humans are sure we're accepted and esteemed can we face the relentless daily grind and field the hardest rocks life throws at us. Any unbiased observer knows we thrive not only by our brute will but also by the love others have for us and by our love for them. We all know, deep down, that in the end love is what being human is all about.

So, authentic spiritual voices will tell you that you are loved as you are. They also will insist on your need to grow in your own ability to love. They will say things like: "Respect all persons, beginning with yourself. Work for justice and more justice. Show compassion to those less fortunate. Support efforts to lift the vulnerable. Open your heart to everyone. Forgive everyone everything. Love even your enemies." If a voice says these kinds of things, you can know it has your best interest in mind. By contrast, you can tell a voice is fraudulent and will harm and even destroy you, if it says things like, "Live only for yourself. Don't let others see the real you. Manipulate those you work with for your own benefit. Despise people you can't control."

So what voices do you hear that must be tested?

If you're like most people, the bothersome voice of conscience talks to you. That's generally a sign of mental health. You've heard the saying: "Let your conscience be your guide." There are problems here. First, you can ignore your conscience. Famous ventriloquist Edgar Bergen once asked his dummy, Charlie McCarthy, "Does your conscience ever tell you what to do?" Charlie snapped back, "Yes! And then I tell **it** what to do!"

Second, your conscience also can be misdirected; it is pliable and unreliable. History tells us that some German children, reared on anti-Semitic diatribes by Hitler and on their parents' bigoted slurs, were nagged by a guilty conscience, because they did not hate or want to hurt their Jewish playmates. If not informed, enlightened and aligned with *agape*, conscience can mislead us.

Most of us, no matter what our age, hear our parents' voices, whether they are still alive or not. Their messages, buried and echoing in our brains since we first heard them as children, still tell us what-to do—or perhaps, most often, what not to do. Sometimes they talk truth and may be helpful. But some things they say aren't true, and we ought not to follow them. You've read it here—I am the Presbyterian minister who says: "Sometimes it's good to disobey your parents."

Nature speaks to most of us. You may hear its *voice* in sunrises and sunsets, in the stars on a crisp, dark night, in thunder and lightning, and in rainbows. These voices may resonate deeply within you and touch you with their ethereal beauty and their uncanny ability to speak "the universal language older than words." If nature simply pleases your best sensibilities with what it says to you, that may be reason enough to continue to listen to it. Nature won't and can't direct you toward ethical maturity, but it at least may remind you of your true size and place in the universe, an important reality with which to be in touch. In its clear lack of morality, it indirectly may help you see that if a moral order is be established, it's up to you and your fellow humans.

In a similar way, you may enjoy the arts that speak to you, such as poetry, music, painting, and sculpture. If you take the time to listen carefully to what they say, they often will call out your highest sentiments, change your values and compel you to go in positive new directions. They also may speak to you of sharing beauty or of doing important things for others as well as for yourself.

We all hear voices daily through the communications media. Sometimes they speak truth; sometimes what they say is false, and we're not always vigilant or perceptive enough to discern the difference. Some of these voices simply want to manipulate us for their own gain. Shamelessly, even as they are trying to exploit us, they tell us they have our best interests in mind. Among them are *authentic phonies*— people who really think they are sincere. Slick salespersons, spin-doctor politicians, and some televangelists come to mind. Wise people check such voices carefully.

Friends and peers also speak to us. Every day our social antennae pick up popular opinion and what we call *conventional wisdom*. Whether from family members, friends, neighbors, or coworkers, these voices often want us not to deviate from tradition, or question current mores, or disagree with anyone, or speak our minds when we think unpopular ideas. We should know that when others call us to conform and not rock the boat, they aren't always speaking with our best interests in mind, and won't serve us well.

The voice of reason may speak through any of these sources. And we need to listen to it as a corrective, when we're tempted to believe, by blind faith, a traditional sentimentality. Once again, however, the outer and inner edges of the universe, and we humans deep down, are too mysterious for logic alone. At some point, the telescope and microscope pass their limits, and we are able without them to discover some of our most important truths. We don't easily come by facts in these deeper and outer regions, and even when we find them, we have to interpret them. Sooner or later reason runs into the brick walls of absurdity, internal contradiction, and baffling paradoxes. Is it rational that "to save your life you have to let go of it?" No. Is it logical that "to become wise you must accept how unwise you are?" No. Reason fails to resolve such simple claims as: "There are *no* absolutes" (Doesn't *no* constitute an absolute?). Reason is an important voice, but it is limited.

Many religious people claim to have heard the voice of God, whether through scripture, other people or their own spiritual depths. Some who have said so have made extraordinary contributions to the world at great sacrifice of themselves. I mentioned Gandhi and Martin Luther King Jr. earlier, because we all know their names; but throughout history there have been many more. We recognize their authenticity; we value their contributions; we honor their heroism.

But we've also heard of religious parents who hear God's voice telling them to kill their children. Most of us think that mental illness causes both the hearing of such a directive and the compulsion to follow it. And we hope that if we ever hear people talk about an urge to do something dreadful like that, whether or not we can convince them they are listening to the wrong God, we'll have the wisdom, compassion, and courage to stop them and to see they get professional help.

We've also known kings and queens, czars, dictators, and presidents, who've said that God told them to send their armies or bombers to evil lands to slaughter their wicked inhabitants, soldiers and civilians, men and women, young and old alike. National leaders in biblical times made such a claim, and some of our leaders have made it in our day. I suggest that a God worthy of respect doesn't say such things, and that heads of state who insist their murderous actions have been directed by God must be confronted. Every German soldier in World War II wore a belt buckle on which was written *Gott Mit Uns* (God is with us). We've all judged them and the German citizenry of that time as wrong for walking in lockstep with the genocidal Adolph Hitler. Let our judgment of their actions remind us to make sure that the generations to come have no reason to condemn us for acquiescing to such voices.

I once asked people in a seminar: "How can you ascertain whether an inner voice speaking to you is God?" Some members quickly identified God with the conscience. Others said God speaks through our dreams and we must interpret them carefully and take them seriously. Still others felt that if you listen to a scripture verse or religious music and a chill runs down your spine or tears well up in your eyes, God must be talking to you. A lot of opinions surfaced and we never reached consensus. To close the session, with a straight face I told the group that a deep, mysterious voice had recently wakened me in the middle of the night and said to me: "Never, ever trust voices you hear in the middle of the night."

Can we in fact hear authentic voices from the "Ground of Our Being," transforming voices of grace and truth and hope, voices that challenge, direct and refresh us? I'm convinced we can. But we're also capable of hearing unworthy, inauthentic voices that lead us astray and bring out the worst in us. And we do not do well by ourselves if we try to excuse our ignoble acts by claiming that our conscience, or our parents, or *God*, or … *the Devil made us do it*. It is a simple point: If we want to be whole, we must test voices we hear to see whether they are internally consistent, fit the facts as we know them and ring true to *agape*.

Choose the Best Path For You

Someone has said that being spiritual is like hiking; "It is all about finding and taking the right path." Or, it's like taking the right road when we have a destination in mind. Most of us walk paths others created by their walking. And the roads we travel have been laid out, thoughtfully, for us by other travelers. So, it's obvious the resources you draw on the path, or road, you choose for your walk are critical, because choices have consequences.

Yogi Berra said: "When you come to a fork in the road, take it." Chuckle at Yogi, but realize that his humor highlights your dilemma without helping resolve it; for what you really want to know is *which* road at the fork is the right one to take. In other words, which direction will best put you in touch with life's highest values, will help deepen your capacity to love, will ground, integrate, balance, and liberate you, will bring out the best in you and elevate your spirit? Almost everyone gets lost in such matters. If you are feeling incomplete, empty or confused about which direction to take, look at a few criteria that may help you discern whether a spiritual path is right for you

First, it may be familiar or foreign.

Our three major theistic religions present various forms of spirituality: mystical, contemplative, charismatic, liturgical, theological, *pietistic*, separatist, activist, and escapist. Christianity offers Catholic orders, Orthodox traditions, Protestant liturgies, and the piety of the free churches, plus their maverick sects. Islam requires a daily schedule of prayer for all believers; its Sufi tradition is mystical and features its famous whirling dervish dancers. Eastern philosophies specialize in spiritual disciplines, such as yoga and meditation. New Age believers blend many of those practices with the strange offerings of the occult. Some secular humanist groups offer what we might call spiritual disciplines, or exercises designed to bring mind and body together.

I would argue that each of us is a unique expression of our species and brings to each moment her or his particular genetic makeup, personality, temperament, needs, background, habits, discomforts, and dreams. Any of us, therefore, may find a particular spiritual discipline helpful, or it may leave us cold. A person may try the same practice others say helped them and not find much value, nourishment, or satisfaction in it. If you feel the need for spiritual disciplines and practices at all, I suggest you weigh each one for what positive value it might bring to you.

If you were reared in a religious tradition, you may feel you have a hole in your heart that only can be filled with symbols and practices from your past. Or, by contrast, the spirituality you grew up with may now bore, anger, and repulse you. Or you may have tried many paths and found that none has nourished you. No matter your personal history, if your life is dry, empty, directionless, worn out, and you feel the need for depth and renewal, you must set aside any prejudice, nostalgia or rebellion you've been entertaining and take steps you think will best support your journey toward being a person who is wholly secular and spiritual. Even as you read these words, they may start you down a positive road you have never taken before or even imagined.

Second, the best path for you may be ancient or newly created.

Every day we hear about new spiritual practices that promise to solve all our problems. Sometimes novelty refreshes us. That's the appeal of Pentecostalism; it looks to "the new things the Spirit is doing." But simply because an insight is newly touted, or a new spiritual practice becomes the rage, it doesn't necessarily breed wholeness. Many of us who have been around awhile find that the new things often are "the same old new things," and that, when it comes to spiritual matters, there really is … "nothing new under the sun."

Some spiritual paths have been around for thousands of years. People endorse them because they are familiar and they have stood the test of time. Entering temples in Luxor, Egypt a few years back, I pictured the people who first walked through the same arches thousands of years ago. When I sat down on the same massive stones where they had sat, I became silent, strangely awed by a sense of connection with people who'd pondered life's largest questions as I was doing. In the same way, members of the world's great religions revere their beliefs, rituals and institutions, in part, because they connect them to the distant past. Because the major religions have been around for thousands of years, because they tie spirituality to an eternal God, and because we rightly value the "wisdom of the ages," the case for their validity based on age can seduce us all by itself.

I'm one whose roots go deep into the ancient Hebrew-Christian tradition and who values much of what it offers. I don't believe, however, that anything in it or in the Bible is true or spiritually profound merely because it's been around a long time. Age does not guarantee authenticity or value. Roman Catholic authorities told the sixteenth-century priest Martin Luther he should not challenge the pope, because Church teachings and the papal line went all the way back to St. Peter. Luther allegedly replied, "Ah yes, but just because you can trace your footprints in the snow back to the place from which you came, does not mean you are going in the right direction."

So, because a spiritual principle or practice is either new or old is no reason either to reject or accept it uncritically.

Third, the best spiritual path for you most likely will take one of three forms.

Form One, *mediated spirituality*, focuses on the holy, supernatural God who is the *Totally Other One*. You, as a sinner, must approach this God only through someone whom God has chosen to bridge the gap between the two of you. This form of spirituality is promoted by the ordained clergy in Judaism, Christianity, and Islam—in part, no doubt, because they see themselves as the appointed, legitimate mediators. They tend to love the age-old disciplines that emerge from the scriptures and tradition. They defend them as superior to nonscriptural exercises and find pleasure and fulfillment in leading people in their practices. Because such *mediated spirituality* is rooted in pre- or unscientific understandings both of the world and of human nature, secular critics see the practices associated with it as irrelevant to life in today's world.

Form Two, *unmediated spirituality*, stresses God's abiding presence at the core of your being. It points you to the fertile garden of your interior life, where you can uncover the God within or, in less religious terms, discover your *true self* and find your *bliss*. Eastern paths, Native American worldviews, feminist theologies, New Age teachings, and even some Christian monastic directives espouse some form of unmediated spirituality. They advocate practices such as meditating, contemplating with a mantra, creatively using silence, singing, chanting, doing yoga, studying the Bible inductively, praying, keeping a journal, taking pilgrimages, and trekking the Himalayas. Christians who push unmediated spirituality usually promote it as a means to tap into the Holy Spirit. Critics tend to describe its excesses in terms of emotionalism, *navel-gazing*, or escapism.

Form Three, which I call *social spirituality*, personally challenges me. It stakes out for action, human rights and civil rights abuses, social, political and environmental injustice, imperialism, militarism and war, racism, sexism, ageism and egoism, homophobia, xenophobia, religious and spiritual deadness, economic exploitation, and an unbridled capitalism that ignores and violates the most vulnerable in society. Practitioners tend to be Spiritual Secularists, or kindred spirits. We may observe few or no traditional religious practices, but we believe we touch life's spiritual depths when we pool our resources and in concert do what we can to curb these destructive powers.

The other side to the Form Three coin reads: If you don't do what you know you ought to do on behalf of the common good, your spirit will be strained and stunted, if not aborted. In addition, when you fail to be compassionate or to do the right thing, it is not enough to put a band-aid of spiritual practices on the failure, as that will not heal your inner core.

Spiritual Secularists don't believe in spirituality for its own sake. We recognize the importance of time for silence, of balancing action with quiet reflection on who we are and what we are doing, and of reflecting in community regarding strategies and tactics for waging justice and peace. So when we sense the need, we employ spiritual practices we believe will repair us, make us wiser, stronger in character, more loving, cooler and more collected, and better able to continue contributing toward a better world. Otherwise, we leave them alone. Critics say this form of spirituality wrongly emphasizes *thinking* and *doing* rather than *being*. This criticism doesn't bother us.

The same flexibility that characterizes Spiritual Secularists may play a part in the practices of those committed to mediated or unmediated spirituality. No matter which one of the paths you choose, it's possible you will draw on some measure of all three of them in your spiritual journey, or perhaps even create your own path from some mix of them.

Fourth, a spiritual path that's genuine will help you fulfill your deepest needs, but it may not meet your greatest wants.

If you feel broken, lost, unfulfilled, and going nowhere, it may be the result of always chasing what you want, rather than what you need. A path good for you helps you to see your strengths and potential and leads you toward the growth you need. It also helps you see your weaknesses, blind spots, and past mistakes so you can deal with them more effectively. It will challenge you to accept yourself as you are, but it also will ask you to become more than you are by rethinking both the values and the goals you've set for your life. At the same time, it won't let you become absorbed with spirituality itself, or be comfortably self-absorbed. The best road may not always be easy, but it will be rewarding.

Fifth, the right, or best spiritual path will affirm your highest purposes.

Spiritual yearnings run from healthy and noble to neurotic and shameful. Check yours to see whether they are genuine or superficial. Worthy spiritual paths will lead you to wholeness and joy, if you're willing to search for truth and proactive love. But they will not let you tolerate what ought not to be tolerated; they won't make you feel good if you're following them mainly to impress others; they won't help you succeed in your spiritual quest if your greatest passions are self-serving. And if along the way you abuse people, authentic spiritual exercises won't fill the emptiness or chase away the blues you suffer as a result.

To find a healthy path, you must identify any less than noble motives you may have and any destructive behavior you're engaging in. Once you've done that, you can expect any spirituality worth its salt to:

Help ground, integrate, balance, and liberate you.

Stop you dead in your tracks to check your behavior.

Renew your sense of surprise, wonder and awe.

Get you to check your values, goals and actions.

Add bone, muscle and heart to your character.

Give you energy, strength and guidance.

Help heal wounds from abuse or abandonment.

Challenge and train you to be nonviolent.

Help you protect and nurture the natural environment.

Free you to be hospitable to those different from you.

Increase your ability to contribute to the common good.

Provide healing and energy after you battle injustice.

Call for self-love, if you spend too much time on others.

Help you better serve the love at the center of life.

Sixth, the best path for you will reinforce spiritual laws that make you most human.

A spiritual law, like a physical law, is a predictable constant, something you can count on. One such law concerns material possessions. It knows they can enhance your experience, but it insists you not betray yourself by counting on them to satisfy your spiritual hunger or make you whole.

A related law requires you to give absolute loyalty only to what has absolute value. Once again, I'm talking about the power of *agapaic love,* which determines how human you are and sustains your spirit. The implication is that, if you trust in something to make you whole that only has relative value (a new blouse, computer mouse, house, or spouse), this law will take its toll on you. We might call this the law of *appropriate commitment;* it's akin to the one that says: "Never trade a dime for a nickel because the nickel is bigger."

Another spiritual law is that of consideration. If you spend reasonable time, energy and money on yourself while you also are *considerate* of others ("love your neighbor as you love yourself"), life sweetens. If you ignore, disdain or violate either yourself or others, life sours.

Expressing appreciation stands as another spiritual law. If you maintain gratitude when graced with the gift of life, your spirit will be uplifted. Because you can learn from negative experiences such as sickness, financial losses or undesired changes in relationships, your gratitude for what you learn from them will enrich you. In any relationship, mutual gratitude is a great spirit-booster for both persons. We do well not to ignore the significance of what others give to us. If we take their gifts for granted, we stifle our possibilities for joy.

You may ignore, reject or effectively skirt spiritual laws like these for a while. Over the long haul you can't break them any more than you can break the law of gravity. In fact, as with physical laws, if you violate them they will end up breaking you. By sensitizing you to such laws and getting you to think about the right spiritual road for you, my purpose has been to help you not get lost and avoid carelessly hurting yourself and others.

Underlying all I have said here is my awareness that peoples' sense of spiritual need differ greatly, depending on their backgrounds, relationships, education, mental health, and life circumstances. We all at some time feel empty, disconnected, and flat; and we may look to spiritual practices to connect, fill or lift us. At the same time, I understand that those fortunate enough to have a healthy measure of self-esteem, relationships marked by stable love, basic resources such as shelter, food and transportation, and who operate by a balanced, solid worldview, may find little or no use for what people call spiritual exercises.

If you are looking for spiritual exercises, however, it's good to know you have more resources at your fingertips than the world has ever offered. Every hour, Eastern monks, New Age gurus, psychologists, clergy and self-appointed experts are giving lectures and leading seminars, retreats, and courses on the spiritual life. They also are busy marketing books, videos and CDs. Large sections in bookstores and thousands of Internet websites overflow with resources.

You shouldn't have any trouble finding offers of guidance. I'm sorry to say, however, that some of them are loaded with timeworn cliches, petty moralizing, God-talk that has little connection to reality, and with frothy stuff. Also, the sheer number can be overwhelming, and wading through the choices can be frustrating and produce the very sense of failure and guilt from which spirit is supposed to free us. If you feel the need for more spiritual direction than you have found here, let me encourage you to check with people you respect. Then, I urge you to practice restraint as you navigate your way through what you decide are the best resources available for you.

In this chapter, I've identified six criteria to test spiritual paths you might take. Even as they encourage you to be open-minded, they should help prevent you from letting anyone pull the wool over your eyes. I urge you to review them before going further. The best path for you …

1. May be either familiar or foreign.
2. May be ancient or brand new.
3. May take one of several possible forms.
4. Will address your needs, not your wants.
5. Will affirm the highest purposes for your quest.
6. Will stand by basic spiritual laws that define you.

Question: How would you describe the authentic human? Or, what kind of people are your personal models? Let me tell you about mine.

People travel to wonder at the height of mountains, at the huge waves of the sea, at the long courses of rivers, at the vast compass of the ocean, at the circular motion of the stars; and they pass by themselves without wondering.

St. Augustine

The principle I advocate is this: living a life in which we strive to do the most good and the least harm to ourselves, other people, animals and the environment, through all of our choices—including what we eat, wear and buy; what we do for work and entertainment; and how we participate in society and democracy as citizens, volunteers, and change-makers.

Zoe Weil

To seek God by climbing to heaven or by praying into the distance, to try to win union with God by good deeds, is to ride the waves in search of water, to hunt in the darkness with candles looking for fire.

Barry Wood

There is no justice in the laws of nature, no term for fairness in the equations of motion. The Universe is neither evil, nor good, it simply does not care. The stars don't care, or the Sun, or the sky. But they don't have to! We care! There IS light in the world, and it is US!

Eliezer Yudkowsky

CHAPTER 14:

MODELS OF WHOLENESS

Those Who Inspire Me

Everywhere you look, people are peddling spirituality. You can tell the shallow ones by their preposterous claims and by what their practices do—and *don't* do—for those who adopt them. If you look carefully, you'll also find healthy ways to be spiritual that will help you mature, and point you down a road between an arid secularism and a supernatural, or sentimental, spirituality.

Spiritual enrichment also can come from observing those whose views, values, and practices inspire us. I am impressed, encouraged, and guided by people who care about the broad range of life's concerns and who pursue them thoughtfully. I respect them as authentically spiritual and secular, and find their lives trustworthy measuring sticks by which to check my own life on the road.

The people I deem authentic and worth copying can be recognized by their actions. They typically …

- **Demonstrate respect for the natural realm.** They stand in awe of the universe for its size, ecosystems, uncountable species, beauty, wonders, and mysteries. They celebrate gorgeous sunsets, moon-rises, sparkling stars against a night sky, ocean waves, flowers, succulents, humming-birds, waterfalls, and the glories of our species and of themselves as persons. Rather than despair in the face of the looming climate-change crisis, they take appropriate steps—no matter how minor—to reduce their carbon footprint, and to help revitalize our life-sustaining environment.

- **Make obvious their connection to the human family.** They show respect for all peoples because of our common origin, genetics, struggles, limitations, mortality, and the need for hopeful visions of the future. They know that human life is relational, and facets of their personalities only can be expressed and fulfilled in relationships that are both honest and loving. They see us all on the same journey, in the same boat, and in need of one another. They seek communities that provide them with support, and with helpful rituals and stories that point to the deeper meanings of their lives.

- **Affirm their sexuality and spirituality.** They try to balance the attention they give to themselves as physical and spiritual persons. They recognize the power and complexity of their sexuality, but they refuse to live afraid of it, or dominated by it. They are aware of the conflicts generated by *eros* encountering *agape*. While they value both forms of love, they turn their relationships over to *agape* and try to cultivate a robust, fun-filled, respectful, tender, and passionate sexuality. With great respect for others, they want everyone to have a healthy and joyful sex life.

- **Create, engage, support, and thrive on the arts.** Because they know their spiritual yearnings cannot always be expressed with words, they try to engage music, dance, the fine arts, theater, poetry and various literary forms to express their responses to life's mysteries. As they celebrate life's gifts, they stoke their own creativity to find meaning and add beauty to the world. The most artistic among them look on the creative contributions they make as critical for being fully themselves.

- **Expand their knowledge.** They eagerly consider ideas from other than their own kind. They can let go of the familiar and welcome new ideas without cherishing them for newness alone. They seek to gain knowledge and express wisdom. They may tap the wisdom of the great traditions, but they don't cling to ideas simply because they're old; and they jettison beliefs that don't connect with what they know is real today. Someone else has said of such people: They honor *tradition* as the living faith of the dead; they reject *traditionalism* as the dead faith of the living.

- **Answer the big questions the best they can.** As they develop their own take on things, they look for insights that challenge them to be their best. They reject superstition and take seriously what makes sense to them. At times they believe it is wise to settle for asking questions and not having to have answers. As they hold their beliefs humbly, they risk their ideas in dialogue with others, and they listen, believing that healthy debate nurtures good ideas. They want to see how their own life-stories connect with others' stories and with the great human stories. And if they have children, they teach them how to think, even as they introduce them to their own worldview.

- **Accept polarities, paradoxes and life's contradictions.** They affirm reason even as they recognize its limitations and believe life is too contradictory and mysterious to be captured fully by logic. They believe faith is no substitute for thinking, but that honest faith and doubt encourage good thinking. In response to life's mysteries, they seek rituals that help decipher and reinforce their deepest understandings and values. In the toughest of times they take life, not themselves, seriously. At the same time, they retain their sense of humor. They also celebrate and party robustly.

- **Approach scriptures seriously, or not at all.** They may respect certain insights from "sacred" books, but they don't worship them. They may value certain scriptural myths, but they don't take them literally. They affirm scholarship, academic freedom and scripture tempered by reason, but they are not sure of the value for human well-being of nitpicking every word in holy books. Because most are overwhelmed by the size, cultural differences and complexity of scriptures, they know they can't expect to read them only in English and talk intelligently about them. They also don't say God spoke to them through scripture, when what they heard from it was silly or trivial, or violated the highest values of compassion, peace and justice.

- **Refuse to worship anything of relative value.** They won't place their undying trust in, or give absolute loyalty to, anything but the love I've identified as *agape*. They don't place beyond criticism any idea, person, product, office, or institution, whether in religion, business, science, or government. They believe the state must keep an eye on religion and vice-verse. They also refuse to believe something or follow particular teachings or spiritual paths simply because an authority expects it of them. At the same time, they take seriously truth-tellers, such as the Jewish prophets, Buddha, and Jesus.

- **Work at being narrow-minded about broadminded-ness**. They respect the right of all persons to hold their beliefs. Even if they are not religious, they look on the enduring religions as different ways to explore the mysterious dimensions of reality; and if they are involved in a religion, they support cooperation between their own faith and all others. They bear witness to truths they believe change them for the better, but they don't feel compelled to convert those whose beliefs differ from theirs. At the same time, they see some beliefs as false, some as nonsense, and some as dangerous. And when religious fanatics promote hatred, division and violence, they break the widely accepted taboo against challenging others' beliefs.

- **Seek virtue as they accept their own limitations and failures.** To strengthen their character, they reflect on what truth, justice and love require. They try to be moral and ethical, not for a pat on the back, but because it is right and it enriches them. While they believe in themselves, their self-esteem gives them no illusion of being morally superior to others. They know that like everyone, they often blunder along and fail to stay on course. But when they make a mistake or fall short they can say, "I was wrong and I'm sorry." In the end, despite any darkness they see in themselves, they are self-accepting, because they believe everyone is accepted at the very *ground of being.*

- **Express themselves graciously and honestly.** They stay sensitive to the needs and feelings of everyone they meet, but they seek healthy relationships in which they also can be honest. Because they want people to be real with them, they try to relate to others as true persons rather than as pseudo-persons defined by social roles and infected with the disease to please. So you generally can count on them to mean what they say and say what they mean, with a touch of grace.

- **Accept the responsibilities and enjoy the privileges of being adults.** They adopt interdependence for their adult psychological style, rather than childish dependence or adolescent independence. They take life, including adversity, in stride, always trying to reconcile their reactions to experience with their feelings and beliefs. They try to discern their gifts, develop their skills and work for the common good, as well as enrich their own lives. Confidence in their worth as humans frees them from the terrible burden of selfishness and helps them endure and often overcome adversity. And because they try to live responsibly for what is worthwhile, they feel fulfilled and, as some of them say, *blessed*.

- **Support peacemaking efforts.** They distinguish between peacemaking and peacekeeping that depends on war and on empire building, which includes invasion of other countries. They view such governmental strategies as immoral and counterproductive. They support efforts that promote international interdependence, human rights and peace through instituting justice for the people. Instead of despising and demonizing strangers, people different from themselves, and their enemies, they extend understanding, empathy, hospitality, and radical forgiveness to everyone.

- **Refuse to resort to violence.** As they face complex ethical, social, and political issues, they try to avoid extremes and seek a third, more nuanced way, building where they can on common ground. At the same time, they work against ignorance, fear, discrimination, oppression, hierarchy, and violence. When they dislike what any government does, they speak up and may raise hell about it, while striving to bring about change by supporting nonviolent resistance against it. Yet, even as they take part in resisting the violence of their government, they deal with their own aggressive tendencies and try to cultivate their capacities for nonviolent peacemaking.

- **Try to live simply.** They appreciate material things, but they don't live mainly to accumulate them; and to get more money isn't what drives them. Rather, they try to avoid the burdens of clutter, mindless consumption, unchecked debt accumulation, and, worst of all, being possessed by their own possessions. If they inherit or earn riches, they use significant portions of them, plus their time and energy, to promote and support change on behalf of the common good. They also view their lives and their goods as gifts on loan, and themselves as spiritual stewards of it all in behalf of the common good.

- **Demonstrate compassion for the weak and poor.** Grateful for the gift of life they didn't deserve or earn, they look for ways to ensure that the sick, oppressed, homeless, hungry, and poor do not drop through our available social safety nets. They oppose social and political powers that ignore or abuse the most vulnerable among us. They support laws that provide for living wages and a just distribution of goods, so everyone can have enough. And while they may be convinced that by being empathic and compassionate they are doing what makes human life more human, they do not do it to feel superior to others.

- **Engage the present world, excited by its possibilities.** They don't try to escape present-day problems by pining for the past or daydreaming of the future (including a possible afterlife). Living in the present, they look forward to a humanity that is more compassionate, just, and at peace with itself than it is today—to a world that is whole and not simply, geographically one. This vision does not embarrassed them, because they believe it is based in the reality of *agape*. They find spiritual nourishment in judging their own values by it and calling others to contribute to its fulfillment.

No one, including me, has a final description of spiritual authenticity. Here again, it's your task to test what I say. If my depictions of what I think are the best human models make sense to you, you can ask yourself: How might they affect my being spiritual and secular from now on? If anything in the above list strikes you as false, or unhealthy, or unrealistic, simply cross it out and think of what you might put in its place. You also may want to write your own description of people you respect most highly.

As you already may have concluded, I see most of those who reflect the behaviors I describe here as Spiritual Secularists. I'm not sure I know

anyone who perfectly lives up to the models of behavior I've traced—
few of us meet what we expect even of ourselves. But I think the list
fairly accurately portrays the concerns, aspirations and commitments,
if not always the practices, of those who work at being authentically
secular and spiritual.

A Few Final Thoughts

Science shapes our lives today. We do not live in the Enchanted
Forest of yesteryear. There are no angels and demons determining
our physical and mental health. I have encouraged you, therefore, to
respect the remarkable knowledge we now possess due to the hard and
sometimes brave efforts of scientists. I also have suggested you not
worship science and be leery of secularists who narrow human life to
facts and figures and who are rock-solid certain that those who differ
with them are automatically wrong and stupid.

Given my own attachments to science and reason, you may be
among readers who found my reflections too philosophical, too rational,
too cold, or not spiritual enough. If so, I ask you to remember that,
while I distrust sentimentality and the abuses of emotion, I affirm the
spiritual, including mystery, the power of *agape*, the light of meaning,
and authentic emotion. I also recognize the limits of rationalism and
science. At the same time, I don't apologize for insisting that claims to
spiritual experience pass the test of intelligent, fair-minded scrutiny, and
enrich your everyday experience. And let me suggest that no matter how
strong your distrust of rationalism, you have no excuse for not putting
your large *Homo sapiens* brain to work in determining what is real and
what being fully human requires of you.

For those readers who have never consciously undertaken to develop
a worldview, I've offered a number of checkpoints to help get you started.
Then, after providing some background on the range of ideas in the
worlds of religion, philosophy, and secular science, I laid out my own
worldview, based on an unlikely meshing of the secular and spiritual. I've
tried to show you why this way of looking at things makes sense to me.

Out of respect for you I have at no point told you what to believe.
I have set before you the reasoning and perspectives to which my study

and experiences have led me. And I have not minced words. But my primary purpose has not been to convert or indoctrinate you. I have left your quest for truth entirely up to you. I've wanted you to buy only those notions that deep down you cannot deny, because their ring of truth is so strong. I have wanted to stop you from sliding through life either believing everything and doubting nothing, or doubting everything and believing nothing. Both options are unworthy, because they let you off the hook of having to think and take responsibility for your wholeness.

When you're finished reading, I encourage you to write down in a simple form, perhaps an outline, what you can easily say is basic to your worldview. Start with the three questions we've been dealing with: "Where did everything come from? Why is life such a predicament? What will it take for me to live my best possible life?" If you have been synthesizing your views on important matters for years, you may find this an easy task. If this is your first time at it, you may have to clear your head by tossing out a lot of trash that has accumulated there since childhood. If that change sounds like it could be somewhat painful, keep in mind that it's what you have to go through in order to end up in a much better place.

As you write, you may be tempted to list the things you no longer or simply don't believe. Do that, if you must. But I urge you to move quickly to what you *do* believe and to be as honest with yourself as you can be. As a result, your own rebuilt worldview will help you deepen your sense of being grounded, integrated, balanced, and liberated. And the road you travel for the rest of your life will be marked by depth and breadth, by the richness of secular and spiritual together, and by the balance of grace and truth, all keys to the light and warmth that can make you whole.

INDEX

ABOUT THE AUTHOR

In 1997, Time Warner published Duke Robinson's award-winning book *GOOD INTENTIONS*. This put an end to his always telling people he was a talker not a writer.

In 2000, the paperback version, *TOO NICE FOR YOUR OWN GOOD*, appeared in 12 languages and as an early Kindle book. It continues to sell briskly. His second non-fiction book and novel are listed on the next page.

Robinson graduated in 1950 from Haverford High School on the edge of Philadelphia. He holds a BA degree in philosophy from Wheaton College, near Chicago (1954), and a Masters of Divinity degree from Louisville Presbyterian Theological Seminary (1958) .

He has lived since 1960, in the East Bay of Northern California. From 1968 to 1996, he *pastored* the progressive Montclair Presbyterian Church in Oakland. For several years during that ministry he served as an adjunct professor at San Francisco Theological Seminary, from which he holds an earned doctorate (1979). He also appeared frequently on Northern California television.

Since 2000, Duke has lived in Rossmoor, an active adult community in Walnut Creek, CA, 16 miles east of Oakland. Barbara, his beloved wife of 54 years died in 2008. He now lives with Claire Blue, whom he identifies as the love of his life. He has four mature children, nine wonderful grandchildren and a super-great, great grandson born in October 2012.

OTHER BOOKS BY DUKE ROBINSON

SAVIOR: An Old Notion in a New Novel of Unthinkable Absurdity (2012)

CREATE YOUR BEST LIFE: How to Live Fully Knowing One Day You Will Die (2011)

TOO NICE FOR YOUR OWN GOOD: How to Stop Making 9 Self-Sabotaging Mistakes (2000)

You can help your friends access *A MIDDLE WAY: The Secular/Spiritual Road to Wholeness*, and these other titles, by sending them this direct link: **https://www.amazon.com/author/duke_robinson** or they can type Duke Robinson into the Amazon.com search slot.

These books are available in Paperback and on Kindle.

Made in the USA
San Bernardino, CA
05 April 2014